The Return of the State?

Erhard Eppler

Translated by Allan Blunden

First published in 2009 by Forumpress

Forumpress
c/o The Global Policy Institute
London Metropolitan University
31 Jewry Street
London EC3N 2EY, UK

ISBN: 978-0-9554975-7-5

A catalogue record for this book is available from the British Library.

For further information on Forumpress, visit our website: www.forumpress.co.uk

Cover Design and Layout: Ben Eldridge ben@somethingdesign.co.uk

Printed by Lightning Source www.lightningsource.com

Contents

List of Abbreviations

ARD	*Arbeitsgemeinschaft der öffentlich-rechtlichen Rundfunkanstalten der Bundesrepublik Deutschland –* Consortium of public-law broadcasting institutions of the Federal Republic of Germany
BBC	British Broadcasting Corporation
CDU	*Christlich Demokratische Union Deutschlands –* Christian Democratic Union of Germany
CEO	Chief Executive Officer
CIA	Central Intelligence Agency
CNN	Cable News Network
CSU	*Christlich-Soziale Union in Bayern –* Christian Social Union of Bavaria
DCIS	Democratic constitutional interventionist state
EU	European Union
FDP	*Freie Demokratische Partei –* Free Democratic Party
GDP	Gross Domestic Product
GDR	German Democratic Republic

GNP	Gross National Product
ICE	Intercity-Express
IMF	International Monetary Fund
MP	Member of Parliament
NATO	North Atlantic Treaty Organization
NCO	Non-Commissioned Officer
NGO	Non-Governmental Organisation
NSDAP	*Nationalsozialistische Deutsche Arbeiterpartei* – National Socialist German Workers' Party
OECD:	Organization for Economic Co-operation and Development
PCI	*Partito Comunista Italiano* – Italian Communist Party
PDS	*Partei des Demokratischen Sozialismus* – Party of Democratic Socialism
PMC	Private military companies
PSO	Preventive security order
R&D	Research and Development
RAI	*Radiotelevisione Italiana* – Italian public service broadcaster
SA	*Sturmabteilung* – stormtroopers
SS	*Schutzstaffel* – protective Squadron
SED	*Sozialistische Einheitspartei* – Socialist Unity Party of Germany
SPD	*Sozialdemokratische Partei Deutschlands* – Social Democratic Party of Germany
UK	United Kingdom
UN	United Nations
USSR	Union of Soviet Socialist Republics
UNESCO	United Nations Educational, Scientific and Cultural Organization
US/USA	Unites States of America
WASG	*Arbeit und Soziale Gerechtigkeit – Die Wahlalternative* – Labor and Social Justice – The Electoral Alternative

WDR	*Westdeutscher Rundfunk Köln* – Western German Broadcasting Cologne
WTO	World Trade Organization
ZDF	*Zweites Deutsches Fernsehen* – Second German Television

Chapter 1

The Malevolent State

I. "The state has sought to destroy her life on four separate occasions. But she is stronger." So runs the headline above the sorry tale of the Australian aborigine Molly Kelly in the supplement to the German newspaper *Süddeutsche Zeitung* of 10 December 2004. In the vivid and moving report that follows, we learn that for sixty years the Australian government pursued a policy of assimilating the aborigines into the white population, and that any means to that end was deemed legitimate – including the abduction of children. Time and time again Molly managed to escape forcible assimilation by going on the run, enduring all manner of dangers and hardships.

Trainee journalists are taught that the more precise expression is always to be preferred over the less precise. So why does the headline not read "Molly's will to live was stronger than the Australian government"? Instead it is "the state" as such that threatens Molly's life. And not only is it prepared to use inhumane means to achieve its questionable ends: it actively seeks to destroy the life of little Molly, and **seeks** to do so with relentless persistence – "on four separate occasions". That is what "the state" is like. A malevolent force with designs on our lives, and a fiercely determined one at that, forever returning to the attack. But we can – we must – resist.

"When the state sacrifices innocents", ran the headline above the lead story in the arts review section of the German news journal *Die Zeit* (No.29/2004). The article introduced by this provocative teaser was a sober and workmanlike piece. It discussed an amendment to Germany's Airspace Security Law, stating that "a hijacked aircraft, including one with passengers on board … may be shot down on orders from the Defense Minister if it appears that it may be used as a deadly weapon against other persons". Having examined the arguments for and against, the author of the article concludes "that Section 14, Paragraph 3 of the Airspace Security Law (which permits the shooting-down of an aircraft under these circumstances) may well be justified", particularly since the innocent are going to die anyway.

Of course, the authors of these pieces are not responsible for the headlines. All the major newspapers employ specialists for that job. And whether or not the headline fits the article is of secondary, not to say minor importance to them. What matters is that the headline "hits home", and catches the reader where the psychologically trained specialist expects to find him. And the headline writer knows perfectly well that the word "state" carries a negative connotation. The German term *Rechtsstaat* – meaning "constitutional state" – carries a positive connotation, and *Sozialstaat* – social or welfare state – is likewise seen as a positive thing by most. But *der Staat* – "the state" – is a very different proposition: a sinister system, impenetrable, all-powerful, dangerous. Why would it not sacrifice even the innocent?

Above all else this system is remote and alien. Many people say with pride "This is my city", and a good few would say, of Baden-Württemberg, Saxony or Germany as a whole, "This is my region" or "This is my country". But who ever says "This is my state"? Agreed, it is hard to **love** a state – here Germany's former

Federal President Gustav Heinemann was right – but should a democrat not look upon the democratic constitutional state as his own, the state willed by him as *citoyen*, sustained by his taxes and defended by his hand? So why is this manifestly not the case in Germany? Why does the term "servant of the state" carry a very different connotation now than it did in 19th century Prussia – namely a rather disparaging one? Why can a newspaper publisher count on the interest and approval of his readership when he portrays the state as sacrificing innocents?

II. The form of words that seemed appropriate and effective to the headline writer at *Die Zeit* also serves to draw attention to something that no legislator in history has ever had to consider before: how to defend society against suicide attacks.

Hitherto all security planning has been predicated on the assumption that the aggressor wished to survive. So whether one was dealing with a violent criminal or a hostile state, all efforts were directed towards deterrence, either in the form of legal penalties or military power. But what if the aggressor has no interest in his own survival? Dead men cannot be punished, and those intent on dying cannot be deterred by the threat of deadly force. Hence the fact that the German *Bundestag* approved an amendment to the Airspace Security Law that would have seemed madness prior to 11 September 2001: that the German Air Force is permitted to shoot down hijacked passenger aircraft that have manifestly been turned into flying bombs. The state, which has an obligation to protect the lives of its citizens, must now actually shorten those lives by a few minutes. The then German Defense Minister Peter Struck declared that he would resign immediately after giving such an order, should he ever be forced to do so. He was making the point that what was being asked here of a fallible human being was so monstrous that he could not continue to live with it and carry on working as before. So a new form of non-state violence presents the state with unprecedented challenges, and places a burden that is sometimes intolerable on the people who serve it. The state is not only unpopular: it is also indispensable. It is not only in bad repute: it is called upon to make good in an entirely new way. For what is at stake in the 21st century is nothing less than its monopoly on the use of force – and thus its very existence.

III. That the state is up against it in the 21st century will not surprise anyone who looks back on the history of the 20th century. The further we move away from this, the century of the nation-state, the more incomprehensible the slaughter of the last two world wars must seem to us; and the more discomfited we are to note how the state monopoly on the use of force degenerated – and not just under Adolf Hitler and Joseph Stalin – into a monopoly on murder, how often the state became an instrument of terror. The 20th century was a century of violence, of state-directed violence, of executive power that got out of hand.

When a hundred US soldiers are killed by insurgents in Iraq in the space of a month, support for the war at home in America starts to crumble. In the First World War an average of 250 soldiers died every hour: Russian, French, German, British, Italian, Serbian, Hungarian, American – every hour for four and a quarter years. France, with 40 million inhabitants, lost 1.7 million of its young men, or more than 4 per cent of its population. Germany lost 2 million out of 70 million, or around 3 per cent. The slaughter of Verdun, where General Erich von Falkenhayn committed vast quantities of men and resources in a bid to "bleed the French army to death", was not a sufficient deterrent to avert the Second World War, which cost the Soviet Union alone more than 20 million lives. The hourly death rate was around one thousand: military casualties, civilians killed by bombing – and murder victims.

And what is even harder to understand today is this: the relatives of the victims, particularly the mothers and wives of the soldiers, endured unspeakable suffering, they wept, many of them broke down – but they did not protest. In Germany many a grieving parent made a point of noting, in obituaries, that they mourned their sons "in proud sorrow".

How were such things possible in a Christian, enlightened Europe? The state had allied itself with a nationalism which, especially in Germany, took on the characteristics of a substitute religion. War was no longer, as it had been in the 18th century, a matter for ruthlessly drilled mercenary armies, but a matter for entire peoples, who had it drummed into them, day after day, that their very survival was at stake. Nobody questioned the right of the state, the nation-state, to send whole generations to their slaughter. The pacifists who did express doubts were a tiny minority, marginalized and persecuted.

And today? If the number of US war casualties ever exceeded the current number of victims of violent crime back home in the USA, the American public would simply not accept it. Of course, nobody puts it in those terms in the US media: but the comparison serves to show that we now have a lower tolerance of war casualties abroad than of crime victims at home.

In Russia, where many millions of young men gave their lives between 1941 and 1945 in order to drive the German invaders from their country, the mothers of military conscripts now take to the streets if they feel that the lives of their sons are being needlessly put at risk. The nation-state has survived the 20th century. But its power to bind people together is diminished. The human right to life and freedom from harm now weighs more heavily in the balance, and it can no longer be so easily canceled out by what governments choose to define as the national duty or the national interest. This is one of the reasons why wars between states are becoming less common. On the other hand, people now accept that forms of non-state and stateless violence are proliferating. The gun lobby in the United States cares little that free access to handguns claims more victims at home than military interventions overseas.

IV. With every passing year that separates the thoughtful observer from the 20th century, it is becoming increasingly easy to see how closely the two world wars are bound up with the breakdown of civilization that state terror represents. This is not a reference to the truism that the war-weary Europeans were dragged into the Second World War by a "Greater Germany" forced to march to the beat of Hitler's drum, but a reminder of what both world wars have in common with Nazism and Stalinism: the devaluation of human life. It was no coincidence that the National Socialist German Workers' Party (NSDAP) attracted many ex-soldiers who had fought in the front line in the First World War; together with even more who came along too late – because they were too young – to perform acts of heroism, but who, by the same token, had never learned what war is really like. Anyone who had seen how hundreds of thousands of German and French soldiers on the Western Front had been torn to pieces or mutilated by heavy guns whose crews never saw the victims of their actions either ended up a broken man, or had to get used to the idea of killing on an industrial scale. A human life more or less: what difference did it make?

In the summer of 1934, when I was seven, I was trailing along behind two men who were walking in the Black Forest. One of them was my father, a mathematician, who liked to read Kant in the evenings. As I listened to their talk, I kept hearing the words "shoot", "shot" and "firing squad". That evening, thoroughly confused, I asked my father what he and his cousin had been talking about. He replied: "Well, my boy, we were talking about June 30th, but I can see that we probably should not have." Perhaps the wave of purges unleashed on 30 June 1934 was one of the connecting links between world war and state terror. The manner in which Hitler, a year and a half after becoming Chancellor, and in his capacity as "the German nation's supreme judicial authority", as he later put it, got rid of troublesome *Sturmabteilung* (SA) leaders, along with conservative figures who had fallen out of favor – including his predecessor as Chancellor General Kurt von Schleicher together with his wife – would probably have been greeted, still, with horror and outrage in Otto von Bismarck's day. But now, fifteen years after the end of the war, the Germans were less interested in the barbaric method – illegal liquidation – than in the outcome: a few SA thugs less. The regular army, the *Reichswehr*, took delight in the defeat of its rivals, and accepted the death of General Schleicher. Less than six weeks later, when *Reichspräsident* Paul von Hindenburg had died, *Reichswehr* generals drafted the notorious oath by which every soldier was individually required to swear "unconditional obedience" to Schleicher's murderer. The fate of the nation was at stake, after all. What did a few murders matter?

Without the devaluation of human life in the First World War it would be difficult to comprehend the National Socialist dictatorship, which in turn led to the Second World War. At its end in 1945, when hundreds of soldiers were hanged from trees and the horrific images from the concentration camps were shown in the cinemas, mankind had reached rock bottom: not since the Thirty Years War had human life been so utterly devalued.

V. All this had to do with the state, or more precisely, the nation-state. But what kind of a state was it that managed to discredit the very idea of the state down to the present day?

To begin with, not only was it not a democracy, it had no desire to be one. "In a democracy I used democracy to get rid of democracy", mocked Hitler. Democracy was old-fashioned, outdated, decadent. Now it was the turn of the *Führerprinzip*, the leadership principle. One man gave the orders, the rest had to obey. The principle applied not only in the government, which no longer met. What was the point of meetings, if there was nothing more to discuss? The *Führerprinzip* also applied at the provincial level, in the so-called *Gauen*, where the Party organization was headed by a *Gauleiter* and the administration was run by a *Reichsstatthalter* (provincial governor). And on down to district (*Kreis*) level, where the *Kreisleiter* ruled like some kind of petty prince. Consequently the atmosphere of a given locality depended to a very large extent on the personality of the

Kreisleiter. These figures ranged from eccentric but honest idealists, to whom the local butcher's wife could complain in confidence – and not in vain – that the boss of the (municipal) abattoir was discriminating against their business, to outright thugs, like Party comrade Hans Rauschnabel in the university town of Tübingen, who was the occasion of a dispute among local intellectuals as to the true meaning of his name: was it *Rauh-Schnabel* ("rough beak"), or *Rausch-Nabel* ("off his head-navel")? Either suited the man. Even at parish level the *Führerprinzip* still applied. There was still something resembling a parish council, but it was no longer made up of elected representatives of the people. Instead it consisted of nominated Party members, whose function was purely advisory.

And yet the state of public administration in Germany, under the totalitarian rule of the *Führer*, was more chaotic than at any time before or since. It was seldom clear who was responsible for what. For alongside the *Kreisleiter* there was also – as there has always been – a *Landrat*, the chief administrative officer for a rural district. While the general principle was that the Party gave orders to the state, it remained unclear where and through whom this was supposed to happen. So the *Landrat*, who, while a Party member, was essentially a public administrator who did things by the book, attempted to perform his duties as before, attending to the upkeep of the roads in his district – very few new roads were built – or looking for good teachers for the village school. But if he was unlucky the *Kreisleiter*, egged on by some local Party branch leader, would interfere whenever he saw fit. Whereupon the *Landrat* would have to withdraw an order or retract a nomination. Soon the local population itself no longer knew who was in charge – the rural district office or the district Party headquarters. The same chaos ruled at every level of administration, from province (*Gau*) down to parish. Even the *Reich* government, so-called – i.e. the various government ministries that continued to function as before – had constantly to reckon with interference from the Party, often in the person of

Hitler's private secretary Martin Bormann. And the ministries did not always cave in to Party pressure. There were arguments, and decisions were put on hold. In short, a less efficient system of government and administration it would be hard to imagine.

VI. This is why historians and sociologists today talk about the Third *Reich* as a *Doppelstaat*, two states existing in parallel: a "normative state" and a "prerogative state". The normative state relied primarily on old-school administrative officials, who for the most part were servants of a regional government rather than the centralized *Reich*: their allegiance was to Prussia, Bavaria, Saxony, Baden, or to the local parish that employed them: Cottbus, Münster, or Grossaltdorf in some remote corner of Württemberg. They had all learned to follow the letter of the law, to treat all citizens alike, whether they were known to be Nazis or not. They took it as a matter of course that the mentally ill were to be properly treated and cared for, that the fire brigade would turn out to attend a fire, regardless of whether it was in the district Party offices or in the local synagogue.

But the Party, and later on more especially the *Schutzstaffel* (SS), sought to exercise control by interfering with the workings of this "normative state". It imposed decrees that ran counter to recognized legal norms, none of which had been officially suspended. It decreed, for example, that on 9 November 1938 fire brigades could only go into action if buildings adjacent to synagogues were at risk; and that the mentally ill must be taken from the asylums and hospitals and gassed. Opponents of the Nazis were lucky if they were sentenced by a regular court under National Socialist laws, rather than simply being carted off to a concentration camp. A man like Fritz Erler, a German politician, probably only survived the National Socialist state because he was sentenced by a regular court to a long-term of imprisonment. The normative state, even though its norms were adapted over time to the wishes of the Party, at least remained predictable. The prerogative state – symbolized by the concentration camp – was entirely unpredictable and governed by a barbarous despotism. It was without legal foundation, and therefore conducted its business away from the public gaze. The existence of concentration camps, and what went on there, was shrouded in mystery. There were whispered rumors, but for the media the subject was strictly taboo. The only people who knew about the gassing of the mentally ill were those who heard in church about the letters of protest written by Bishop Theophil Wurm.

It was only in the early years of National Socialist rule that the prerogative state attempted to cloak itself in the appearance of legality. As when, for instance, on the day following the *Reichstag* fire, the – democratically elected – *Reichspräsident* suspended all key civil liberties. Or when a supine *Reichstag* was permitted to pass a retrospective law declaring the murders of 30 June 1934 and the two days that followed to be "legitimate" on the grounds of "national self-defense". But in point of fact these supposedly legitimate "measures" had not been carried out by the police, as the authority responsible, but by the SS. And the legal system had made no provision for the SS.

In 1935 discrimination against the Jews was given a "legal basis" in the Nuremberg Race Laws. Anyone could see that this marked the end of a legal tradition dating back almost 150 years. The principal aim of the Laws was doubtless to force the Jews to leave the country by making life unpleasant for them. There was no mention of murder, of course. That was strictly the province of the prerogative state, which not only avoided the outward forms of legality, but now increasingly shunned the public gaze.

The longer the National Socialist regime lasted, and the closer it came to final defeat, the more the normative state was colonized and infected by the prerogative state. In the end not even a semblance of legality was maintained, despite the fact that the Weimar Constitution had never been officially annulled. What is remembered is the arbitrary despotism and the rule of terror of the prerogative state.

VII. Anyone who regularly attended Protestant churches and church synods in the German Democratic Republic (GDR) could not help noticing how often the word "state" came up in conversation. "The state has offered", "the state has prohibited", "the state fears", "the state suspects", "the state would like" – and so on. If one asked exactly who the state was in any of these instances, one got very different answers. "The state" could mean – as one might most plausibly infer – the State Secretary for Church Affairs, who for many years was a certain Klaus Gysi. But it could equally well mean the district secretary of the Socialist Unity Party of Germany (SED), or the local Party secretary, or even a *Stasi* officer. One person it never turned out to be, curiously, was the Minister for Culture and Education, Margot Honecker, because she never spoke to the churches. Although on one occasion, in 1979, it was her husband, the General Secretary and Chairman of the GDR's Council of State, who met with church leaders.

But why did the theologians not just say "The State Secretary wants us to …", or "The SED requires", or "Our local Party secretary is threatening to …"? The explanation may lie within Lutheran theology itself. The people to whom the church was speaking were all representatives of "those in authority over us", to whom the Christian owed obedience (according to St. Paul, *Romans*, Chapter 13), even if they had made atheism the official state doctrine. Acknowledging the authority of the state was part of Lutheran tradition. Consequently the GDR leadership had very little trouble with the most conservative Lutherans. What Paul had **not** written, either to the Romans or to the Corinthians, was that one should be subject to an official state party.

But there were other reasons too. In the National Socialist state the bishops or church councils had known very well whether they were dealing with a Party official or someone from the Ministry of Church Affairs. They still retained a vestige of that trust in state officials – even if they were wearing a Party badge – which had grown up over the centuries between church and state, and which was still extended to Paul von Hindenburg. But the NSDAP, even though it was the only official state party, remained an organization whose "world view" stood revealed, more clearly with each passing year, as anti-Christian. They were prepared to take orders from the former, but not from the latter. And often enough they were able to exploit conflicts between the two. Or as a historian would say today: between the normative state and the prerogative state.

This divided state-within-a-state did not exist as such in the GDR. For one thing, there was no charismatic leader who could issue orders without regard to the law, whose word **was** the law: but instead a *Politbüro* that met regularly once a week, passed resolutions and issued instructions to the government. Needless to say, these instructions were obeyed by the People's Chamber as well, not to mention the Party Congresses. But at least the People's Chamber enshrined the will of the *Politbüro* publicly in the form of laws and resolutions, which may not always have accorded with our notions of legality, but which did at least clarify where people stood in relation to the law. When emigration from the GDR was made a statutory offence, this was clearly a denial of the basic human right to freedom of movement; but with the passing of this law everyone at least knew what to expect if they tried to flee the country and failed. The East German state was more predictable than the National Socialist state. The SED had co-opted the legal and administrative system to its purposes more systematically and thoroughly than the NSDAP. So it had no need of a parallel "prerogative state".

Every schoolboy knew what the Marxist view of the "*bourgeois* state" was. The state was the tool of the ruling class, the *bourgeoisie*. But it could equally well serve as the tool of socialism, at least for an extended transition period. It was this socialist state that the churches felt they were dealing with, regardless of whether they were meeting the State Secretary or the district Party secretary. Only a handful of shrewd political operators such as the Head of the Secretariat of the Federation of Evangelical Churches Manfred Stolpe could venture to extract advantages for the churches from the differences of opinion, and above all the vanities, that divided functionaries and organizations.

VIII. What did the population of the GDR feel about this state? Certainly there was only a small minority that truly believed in it and actively supported it. Another, and possibly even smaller, minority hated it, resisted it, and wanted to be rid of it as quickly as possible. But where did the great majority stand?

The majority put up with it, distrusted it, just as it, the state, distrusted them. At the end of the day this state was willed into being by the occupying power. The majority came to terms with it and got used to the idea that the state was in charge of everything – and therefore responsible.

This was no longer the "father state" that the Germans had for so long loved to invoke. This was more like the "stepfather state". Somehow people never quite warmed to it: they made fun of it sometimes, occasionally wished it to the devil, tuned in to the TV broadcasts from another state at 8.00 p.m. and put their trust, when push came to shove, in that other state's currency. But they acknowledged that the stepfather fulfilled his obligations towards the children he had acquired through marriage – without exciting any great outpourings of gratitude. He was required to provide them with secure employment, which had to remain secure even if they did not exert themselves unduly. He was also responsible for providing cheap rents with heating and hot water included, even if this meant that the housing stock could not be maintained and repaired. And of course pensions and health insurance. If the economy was in trouble, it was the fault of the state, because all the businesses were state-owned. Author Landolf Scherzer has described how an SED Party secretary worked himself into the ground to achieve just a fraction of what the market, elsewhere, sorted out without missing a beat.

And all the time the SED knew very well that custom and habit had bred a sense of entitlement. Members of the Central Committee, when challenged about the profligate waste of energy that resulted from the system of cheap rents with heating costs included, replied that this was a landmark social achievement that one was well advised not to tinker with. And if one complained to them about the foul, stinking lakes of liquid manure outside the pig fattening units, they simply replied that the environment was less important than making sure that everyone had cheap pork on the dinner table. The stepfather dared not impose privations on his stepchildren that they might have understood and deplored as a neglect of his duty of care.

So on the one hand the "stepfather state" in the GDR was an object of distrust and often contempt, while on the other the majority expected the stepfather to provide a degree of care and all-round support that a reasonable "father state" cannot allow his children to enjoy, if only because it would set a bad example.

After reunification the liberated stepchildren gave the newly enlarged German Federal Republic a substantial vote of confidence in anticipation. But this soon melted away when the new "father state" showed itself neither willing nor able to provide what they had come to expect from their stepfather. What is more, reunification became possible at the very moment when the moderate German model of capitalism was being superseded by a more Anglo-Saxon model, which, driven by the need to compete globally, took on a predatory aspect. Consequently many card-carrying East German citizens think they exchanged their stepfather for the father from hell.

Matters were not helped by the naivety of the Federal government of the day, which simply left the business of reunification to the market and the bureaucrats. It never even posed the political question: What should the Germans actually do now – together – with the gift of union, which, it seems, had not so much fallen into their lap as landed on their head. Instead they dispatched officials to the East, whose task it was to teach the dazed and bewildered locals how to organize a tax office or a rural district office, and which statutory provisions were to be observed when. The longed-for united state turned up in the shape of bureaucrats of varying sensitivity. No wonder only a minority accepted this state as their own.

IX. What the older generation experienced and suffered in their state and through their state, and in some cases what they themselves contributed to that experience and that suffering, gets passed on to the younger generation at the dinner table, in the pub, but also in the classroom and lecture hall: and the young listen with incredulous amazement, and often with distaste, to these accounts, some of which are more accurate than others. But it is a different story when we turn to literature, where writers have given expression to their horror of the all-powerful state that rules by war and terror. One work that resonates particularly here is George Orwell's *Nineteen Eighty-Four*, which influenced the way many Europeans thought and felt in the second half of the 20th century – and often the way they acted politically as well. Written in 1948, the novel still reads today like a bad dream from which one longs to awake. It is no coincidence that this dystopia of totalitarian tyranny was published shortly after the Second World War, when Stalinism had triumphed along with Stalin's armies, and even the Allies were stunned by the monstrous crimes of the German prerogative state.

In Orwell's Oceania the prerogative state swallowed up the normative state, just as it had in the final days of the Nazi regime. Winston Smith, the novel's main character, concluded that nothing is illegal, not even the keeping of a diary, for the simple reason that there are no laws. But of course a diary counts as a "thoughtcrime" and is punishable by death. Where there are no laws and consequently no concept of legality, the individual is constantly at the mercy of those in power.

In the – top secret – notes of Emmanuel Goldstein, the evil enemy, who is the daily target of the "Two Minutes Hate", we read: "In Oceania there is no law. Thoughts and actions which, when detected, mean certain death are not formally forbidden, and the endless purges, arrests, tortures, imprisonments and vaporizations are not inflicted as punishment for crimes which have actually been committed, but are merely the wiping-out of persons who might perhaps commit a crime at some time in the future." (George Orwell, *Nineteen Eighty-Four*, London 1989, p.220)

The Party, which decides who may live and who may not, uses the "Thought Police", who do not even trust the employees of the "Ministry of Truth", where Winston Smith works. Naturally this Ministry does not serve "truth" as we understand the term, but rather has the task of constantly redefining what truth is, entirely without regard to any facts as such, so that Winston – either by way of disguise or as a cynical joke – invents his own hero figure, one Comrade Ogilvy. He gives him the life-story of one who is an example to others, which of course has to be consistent with the war that Oceania wages some of the time against Eastasia, but currently against Eurasia. "At the age of three Comrade Ogilvy had refused all toys except a drum, a sub-machine gun and a model helicopter. At six – a year early, by a special relaxation of the rules – he had joined the Spies; at nine he had been a troop leader. At eleven he had denounced his uncle to the Thought Police after overhearing a conversation which appeared to him to have criminal tendencies. At seventeen he had been a district organizer of the Junior Anti-Sex League. At nineteen he had designed a hand grenade which had been adopted by the Ministry of Peace and which, at its first trial, had killed thirty-one Eurasian prisoners in one burst. At twenty-three he had perished in action. Pursued by enemy jet planes while flying over the Indian Ocean with important dispatches, he had weighted his body with his machine-gun and leapt out of the helicopter into deep water, dispatches and all – an end, said Big Brother, which it was impossible to contemplate without feelings of envy. Big Brother added a few remarks on the purity and single-mindedness of Comrade Ogilvy's life. He was a total abstainer and a non-smoker, had no recreations except a daily hour in the gymnasium, and had taken a vow of celibacy, believing marriage and the care of a family to be incompatible with a twenty-four-hour-a-day devotion to duty. He had no subjects of conversation except the principles of Ingsoc, and no aim in life except the defeat of the Eurasian enemy and the hunting-down of spies, saboteurs, thought-criminals and traitors generally." (ibid., p.49)

This idealized biography, invented by the hero of the novel, Winston Smith, shows in caricatured form what this state expected from its subjects – and was able to exact from them.

X. Where the state decrees what is truth, it inevitably finds itself in difficulties when the political constellation alters and the designated enemies and objects of hate change. Thus the Nazi propaganda machine struggled, between August 1939 and June 1941, to explain to the Germans why the Soviet Union had been "world enemy No.1" up until 22 August 1939, in thrall to "Jewish Bolshevism", then from one day to the next became a partner and friend in the fight against Western "plutocracies", only to revert, after 22 June 1941, to being the repository of all evil, an abomination that must be destroyed.

So it is that in Oceania history must be continuously rewritten. And the authorized version is always the most recent one. "The mutability of the past", concludes Goldstein, "is the central tenet of Ingsoc" – the state-imposed view of the world that purported to be English socialism. The past must always be what the Party wants it to be. "This holds good even when, as often happens, the same event has to be altered out of recognition several times in the course of a year." (ibid., p.222)

Not only have laws been abolished, but also "truth" as it has been understood, sought after and respected since the beginning of human time. But the search for truth is the attempt to lay hold of reality, to "grasp" it in every sense; so when truth flies out the window, reality necessarily follows.

Of course George Orwell, who had already published a brilliant essay on political language in 1946, knew perfectly well that if you want to destroy the truth, you must begin by destroying language. And in the Oceania of *Nineteen Eighty-Four*, this is done with ruthless thoroughness. For Orwell, this aspect of his dehumanized dystopia was so important that he adds a 15-page appendix to the novel devoted to "Newspeak". "Newspeak, indeed, differed from almost all other languages in that its vocabulary grew smaller instead of larger every year. Each reduction was a gain, since the smaller the area of choice, the smaller the temptation to take thought. Ultimately it was hoped to make articulate speech issue from the larynx without involving the higher brain centers at all." (ibid., p.322)

Thoughtcrimes punishable by death would become impossible simply because the words to express them would no longer exist. "Countless other words such as honor, justice, morality, internationalism, democracy, science and religion had simply ceased to exist." (ibid., p.318) And the word "free" was only used in the sense of "free from lice". (ibid., p.313)

Since works written in traditional English could not be translated into "Newspeak", intellectual history as such was extinguished at a stroke. There was no tradition, no history – just an "endless present". Thus was the principal goal of the State Party achieved: "To extinguish once and for all the possibility of independent thought." (ibid., p.201)

Not only thoughts, but also emotions were to be reduced to what served the interests of the State Party: hatred, fear, rage, triumph, self-abasement. (ibid., p.279) Consequently the love between Winston and Julia had to end with the annihilation of the lovers. But annihilation did not just mean death. That was not enough for the new rulers. First of all the individual had to be broken, transformed into a cringing, whimpering animal by torture. So in the end the two lovers betrayed each other. They were not permitted to die as lovers. Otherwise the triumph of the state would have been less than complete.

XI. The argument about whether Orwell's vision of a totalitarian state that eradicated every vestige of humanity owed more to the victorious Soviet Union or to Hitler's shattered *Reich* is fairly pointless. With remarkable acuity Orwell took his analysis of both systems to its logical conclusion. And since he was a creative writer he did not content himself with abstract insights: two years before his early death he wrote the most memorable and influential dystopia of the twentieth century. Whether the perfect apparatus of power envisaged by Orwell can still be called a "state" is a question to which we shall return later.

When the year 1984 finally dawned, the world, and especially Europe, was further removed from Orwell's vision of horror than it had been in 1948. Spain, Greece and Portugal had become democracies, and Germany now had a sustainable democratic government. Six years later communism imploded, without serious resistance from those who were ousted from power. Nobody will ever be able to say what part George Orwell's warning vision played in this very different historical outcome. What is clear is that the images of the Orwellian dystopia have penetrated so deep into the European consciousness that they have survived both Nazism and communism. Hitler and Stalin belong to history; they are closed chapters in the history of Europe. Orwell and his influence live on.

And I am not talking about a minority of intellectuals who, when the European interior ministers say that thumbprints in our passports would help in the fight against crime, immediately invoke Orwell. I am talking about our collective relationship with the state. Confronted with an institution that tends toward the excesses described by Orwell, we are well advised to adopt an attitude of extreme caution, not to say defensiveness and suspicion. Of course, only a few have drawn from Orwell's premonitions the inference that we are really better off without the state at all. But it is probably a majority of Europeans who are fearful about the state becoming too powerful, while so far only a tiny minority fears that it could become too weak or indeed impotent – and perhaps already has.

Profiting from these fears are forces to whom Orwell certainly never wished to give succor: those rulers of globalized corporations who can only smile with amusement at the checks to which a democratic head of government in Europe is subject, who by the mere threat of **not** doing something – namely investing – can exert more influence on fiscal legislation than government finance ministers, or indeed 600 members of parliament.

Of course it is principally historical experience that teaches us to regard the threat of the all-powerful state as greater than that of the impotent state. But the horrific images in which one of the cleverest Europeans of the 20th century embodied this experience will surely continue to affect generations who have grown up in well-ordered democratic constitutional states. The newspaper headline quoted at the beginning of this chapter – "The state has sought to destroy her life on four separate occasions" – could equally well be referring to Winston Smith's Julia. But the follow-up line – "she is stronger" – is not remotely applicable to her. Nobody can stand up to Orwell's totalitarian Oceania. Not only does this state **want** to destroy every vestige of individuality, it has the power to do so. This is what distinguishes it from the "totalitarianism" described by political theorist Hannah Arendt. And this is what explains the enduring political impact of Orwell's *Nineteen Eighty-Four*.

Chapter 2

The Stripped-Down State

I. Germany's student rebellion of the late 1960s can probably be seen as a delayed consequence of 20th century state terror. Dismayed and disgusted, the young generation compared their unassuming, democratically adjusted parents and grandparents, averse to excess in all its forms, with the things that these same good citizens had failed to prevent, had indeed allowed, tolerated, aided by their conscientious labors, facilitated by looking the other way – even actively perpetrated. This fed much of the anger with which they now sought to clear the board and start again.

And because they saw no clear break between the world that came to its terrible end in 1945 and the new world that began in 1949, they hurled their accusation of fascism against the new Federal Republic – which hurt those people the most who had risked their lives to oppose the Nazis, and who were now in positions of responsibility. The hatred of many of the young rebels was directed against the Federal Republic, which they denounced as a cleverly disguised continuation of Hitler's *Reich*. And since they broke the laws of this state from time to time, they soon got to know it from its uglier side, with its water cannon, its clubs, its rubber truncheons and, in the case of student Benno Ohnesorg, its firearms.

For them this state was first and foremost an instrument of repression and subjugation, in the service of monopoly capitalism. What they saw in this state was not a mission – not even the mission to reform – but an enemy. The monopoly on the use of force which this state, like all others, claimed for itself and defended was felt by many – and not just by Red Army Faction terrorists Andreas Baader and Ulrike Meinhof – to be the tool of a regime that was essentially illegitimate.

It is one of Willy Brandt's great achievements that he was able, in the early 1970s, to bring into the SPD a small section of the student revolt that was open to the possibility of politics, and to integrate them gradually, with great patience and some humor, into the political system of the Federal Republic. It should be pointed out that this was not achieved without endless trouble, and that Brandt came in for a great deal of criticism, not least from members of his own party.

During the famous "march through the institutions" it was the marchers who changed more than the institutions, of course. But one of the things that proved most enduring among the generation of 1968, at an emotional level if not intellectually, was their relationship to the state.

The difficulties that this generation – most strongly represented later on among the Greens – had with German reunification doubtless stemmed primarily from their unease about the state, which was more emotional than rational in character. Now this state was about to get even bigger, and to embrace people who were just then in the process of constructing something of their own, something better, on the ruins of the SED state. This is why many people talked about the impending threat of another "Greater Germany", which said a great deal about their knowledge of history, but nothing at all about the choices that had to be made in 1990.

This is not about passing judgment on a generation whose contribution to the political culture of Germany, all things considered, was probably helpful. It is simply an attempt to explain why the debate about the state that is now so badly needed is not coming – cannot come – from the generation of 1968, not even from those now in government. Today many of this generation are neoliberals, and those who are not take the view that a disparaging critique of the state is not the worst thing about neoliberalism.

Many of those who took a strict Marxist line and fought against the state as a tool of the ruling capitalist class now look on with bemusement as this very ruling class attempts to dismantle the state.

II. In April 1947, when George Orwell was busy thinking the totalitarian state through to its logical conclusion, a small group of liberals met in Paris at the instigation of Friedrich August von Hayek. Most of them were economists, whose names were far less well known then than they are now: Ludwig von Mises, Walter Eucken, Karl Popper and Wilhelm Röpke. The 35-year-old Milton Friedman was also there. Together they founded a society to promote the liberal ideal.

And they had good reason. In Europe the era of the war economy was slowly drawing to a close. During the war it was governments who decided what industry should produce: first and foremost, whatever the air force, army or navy had needed. More and better bombers, tanks and U-boat hunters, plus everything else that service personnel need, such as uniforms, blankets, cooking utensils, cigarettes and enough to eat. In Britain food was still rationed in 1947, and because of the coal shortage Labour Premier Atlee even planned to ration hot water – prompting Winston Churchill, then leader of the opposition, to observe waspishly: "then the government has no need to wonder why it is getting increasingly into bad odor."

In Western Europe coalmines, steelworks and banks were nationalized. In Germany social democrats and christian democrats joined forces to get a nationalization clause inserted into the constitution of Hesse.

No wonder liberal economists now reminded us of the benefits of a market economy, waxing categorical on the subject: "The position of the individual and of the voluntary group is being increasingly undermined by the expansion of arbitrary state power."

This now had to end. The "voluntary group" of strong-minded individuals who met in Paris championed the cause of private property and free-market enterprise. And that took some courage back in those days.

It was primarily thanks to Hayek and Friedman that the concerns of this circle gave rise to a doctrine that continues to exert its influence to this day, even in communist China. Propagated by some as pure science, opposed by others as ideology, since the 1980s it has achieved global currency, not to say unchallenged hegemony.

Hayek and Friedman did for the liberal economy what Orwell had done for the totalitarian state: they thought it through to its logical conclusion. Just as the power of the state is seen by Orwell as absolute, or in other words divorced from law, from the will of the citizen, from human dignity, indeed from everything that makes men and women human, their striving for truth, freedom and love; so now the market is seen as absolute, divorced from the ties and demands of the family, religion, the public good, the state, divorced from the human need for justice, care and attention, security and safety.

There is one important difference, however, between the free-market and the totalitarian state. Those who wanted to make the market absolute were neither able nor willing to divorce it from law or from the state that makes the law. No market can function without law, or without an institution that enforces the law. But there was an inbuilt bias towards allowing only as much state as the market needed.

Liberalism wanted to free the citizen – and not just the property-owning *bourgeois* entrepreneur – from the nanny state that thought it should be running everything. Neoliberalism takes the market as its starting point, and rates the value of everything, including the state, in terms of how it serves the market. It is market-radical in its approach.

At the same time the lines of thought pursued by these radical thinkers do sometimes intersect, as when Hayek opines that the very concept of social justice "has been the Trojan Horse through which totalitarianism has entered". (Friedrich August von Hayek, *Law, Legislation and Liberty*, London 1976, p.136) Orwell, better versed in history, would probably have pointed out that this is certainly not true of fascism, while the communists had nothing but contempt for the social democratic illusion of social justice. They were not interested in better social policies: what they wanted was the dictatorship of the proletariat in the shape of their party.

It certainly makes sense that an economist who places total reliance on the market, and for whom the wisdom of the market is far superior to all other kinds of wisdom, should have no use for the concept of social justice. What makes less sense is the argument that the market is all about "impersonal processes" rather than morally relevant events, so that market outcomes cannot be judged in moral terms either – he being of the view that the question of social justice is a moral question.

When Hayek confesses that he cannot think in social terms, and does not even know what that means, this could be dismissed as the usual institutional blindness of the distinguished scholar to what is going on outside his specialist field. By that he doubtless means much the same as former British Prime Minister Margaret Thatcher with her famous comment: "There is no such thing as society". Mrs. Thatcher was not giving lectures, though: she was at the head of an important country – or to be more precise, a great state. But what is the point of the state where there is no society? Is its only purpose to safeguard the market?

The Return of the State?

In a Europe that would be unthinkable without Aristotle, but more especially without the New Testament, such views must invite protest, the protest of those who will not be told, who seriously believe there **is** such a thing as society, especially given that man is a social being. That being so, we have need of people who will look after the wellbeing of this society and take thought for the common good, the *res publica*. Without such people, they tell us, there would be no universities, no professors of economics, not even a functioning market.

Economic theories do not need society, just the market and the individual, an individual who is always out for what he can get, who seeks his own economic advantage – i.e. wants to earn money – and therefore engages with the market as a supplier and consumer. That this person exists – or to be more precise, that something of this person is present in nearly all of us – is not denied even by non-economists. Even a grandmother who has never seen the inside of a university, but has some experience of human nature, will not say otherwise.

But she will ask whether people do not have other interests and inclinations besides: the desire to seek for joy, security and safety as one human being among fellow human beings, to dispose freely of one's time and to take spontaneous decisions that are not necessarily rational. An intelligent economist will not gainsay this. But he will object that it is hardly relevant in economic terms.

The people who set out to reform the fare structure of the German railways in 2003 – probably with the benefit of training in economics – really believed that the Germans had nothing better to do than to be constantly checking how far in advance they had to book a train journey in order to save the maximum amount of money. But the outcome was exactly what experienced rail customers could have told them from the beginning: the big advantage of rail travel, namely that you do not have to decide the night before whether you will take an earlier or a later train, was more important to people. Whereupon bookings for long-

26

distance rail travel in particular simply collapsed. After a bit of self-righteous bluster the fare reformers had to back off.

III. When the image of man is up for discussion, the churches also want to have their say, not least on the subject of neoliberalism. The Christian churches are among those who will not be told, or as Gerhard Willke more grandly puts it: they are "resistant to learning". In his – purportedly critical – account of neoliberalism we read: "The left/socialist and church-based critiques of neoliberalism are in agreement that the market encourages a 'destructive egoism'. Resistant to learning, the churches cultivate the idea of the fundamentally good, socially responsible individual, and look with biblical aversion ('You cannot serve God and Mammon', *Matthew 6*, vv. 24-34) upon an economic order that is founded on – indeed, is presumably designed to produce – the selfish individual." (Gerhard Willke, *Neoliberalismus*, Frankfurt/Main 2003, p.151)

Nobody who has been through confirmation classes or heard mention of original sin or Luther's doctrine of grace is likely to accuse the Christian churches of "cultivating the idea of the fundamentally good (etc.) individual". For two centuries the churches have accused the Left of believing in Jean-Jacques Rousseau's concept of the good man, who only needs to be placed in the right environment for him to act in accordance with his innate virtue. For this and other reasons, Christians were regarded by many lecturers in Marxism-Leninism as deaf to argument and persuasion. And the social teaching of the churches has always preferred the market economy over the command economy. What the churches now fear – and in this they are at one with social democrats – is the commodification of consciousness, which leaves less and less room for religion, or indeed for any preoccupation with the public good. Christians know full well what human beings can become if appeal is made only to their greed and their desire to make money. This is why they distrust an ideology that cannot accommodate the idea of man as a social being because it perceives him only as a creature of the market.

To call the churches "resistant to learning" on that account is clearly to expect them to preach Friedrich August von Hayek rather than Jesus of Nazareth. But that presupposes a claim to truth which, if not quite totalitarian, certainly qualifies as overweening.

IV. One can argue about theories all day long. If necessary it is always possible to find a quotation from the theorists to relativize any abruptnesses and straighten out any obvious distortions. But it is a different story in practice. Here it is easy to tell what kind of person one is dealing with. And this applies particularly to the relationship of neoliberalism to the state.

This difference between neoliberal theory and neoliberal practice, particularly where the state is concerned, has been noted even by Francis Fukuyama. In developing countries especially, he argues, the state should have been supported in many areas and even strengthened in others. "The economists who promoted liberalizing economic reform understood this perfectly well in theory. But the relative emphasis in this period lay very heavily on the reduction of state activity, which could often be confused or deliberately misconstrued as an effort to cut back state capacity across the board." (Francis Fukuyama, *State-Building: Governance and World Order in the 21st Century*, New York 2004, p.5)

Confusion or not, neoliberal practice vis-à-vis the state was and is clearer and more one-sided than neoliberal theory. Even the notorious Washington Consensus of 1989, which is now held responsible for weakening and ruining many states in the southern hemisphere, was no radical pamphlet. The ten-point program as summarized by John Williamson, an economist at the Institute for International Economics, which then became the credo of the World Bank, the International Monetary Fund (IMF) and US government policy towards Latin America, contains nothing that need necessarily have threatened the existence of these states. Since the Washington Consensus is now more often criticized than quoted, here are the ten points:

1. Lowering of budget deficits to a non-inflationary level.
2. New public spending priorities in favor of education, infrastructure, etc.
3. Fiscal reform designed to cut marginal tax rates and broaden the tax base.
4. Transition to market-determined interest rates ("financial liberalization").
5. Exchange rates competitive enough to induce a rapid growth in non-traditional exports.
6. Foreign trade: quantitative restrictions to be abolished, tariffs to be reduced.
7. Abolition of barriers impeding the entry of foreign direct investment.
8. Privatization of state-owned enterprises.
9. Deregulation to encourage start-ups, general removal of restrictions on competition.
10. Better protection for property rights, especially in the informal sector.

What John Williamson had intended as a flexible guideline soon became the model for all developing countries, irrespective of whether they were among the poorest – the least developed countries – or whether they were classed as newly industrializing countries. In the IMF's structural adjustment programs the Washington Consensus was simply foisted indiscriminately on highly indebted countries. The particular circumstances of individual countries were ignored: one knew what was good for them, after all.

It was not only in Nobel Prize winner Joseph Stiglitz that the Consensus soon found a fierce critic. The author himself, John Williamson, now blames the US Treasury, and the Bush administration, for the radicalization and failure of the doctrine. At a conference in Berlin in September 2004 Williamson admitted that after the experience of the intervening 15 years he was now in favor of a more active role for the state. Evidently the effect of neoliberal theory has been to engender a far more radical, market-radical practice.

Of course, Hayek and Friedman were far too intelligent to imagine there could be a flourishing economy without a functioning state. Even the neoliberals know that economic activity is not possible without a clear and enforceable legal order, without internal and external security, without a system for regulating markets and competition. And unless they are completely provincial – which can be the case in Germany – then they will have heard or seen what happens to the economy when a state falls apart and gives way to an *entité chaotique ingouvernable*. But the deviant practice also has something to do with the fact that the theory has blind spots. Practice cannot afford any blind spots.

Take ecology, for instance. It is possible to read quite lengthy neoliberal treatises without ever coming across the word. Or the concept of sustainable development either, even though, ever since the Brundtland Commission of 1987, we cannot imagine political debate without it. There is no way the market is ever going to bring about sustainable development by its own exertions and wisdom, without some sort of ecological ground rules being established by the state. Is an ecological framework for economic activity an unnecessary piece of regulation, a mere hindrance for the market? Apparently former US President George W. Bush thought so. But how representative is he?

Neoliberals quickly agree that too much welfare state is harmful. But just how much welfare state is necessary, justifiable, even perhaps helpful, is only vaguely hinted at. In particular, there is no consideration of what a viable state needs in order to be able to fulfill its minimum obligations, or of what a democratic constitutional state has to do in order to win and retain the loyalty of its citizens. The state as guarantor of the law is simply treated as a given, even though we now know that this can by no means be taken for granted. Let others ponder the role of the state. And that is exactly what they are now doing.

The urgently needed debate about the role of the market, the function of civil society and the duty of the state in a future Europe – in short, about what kind of European model we want to see – is not going to be initiated by neoliberals. But it has to come.

V. The favorite topic of politicians and commentators who support market-radical views is taxation. And the usual starting point for discussion is the massive "government spending ratio". If we add together all government expenditure at the national, regional, district and parish level, plus the cost of statutory social insurance, and express this as a fraction of GDP, the result is the "government spending ratio". This means that as the German population ages, and more money has to be spent on pensions – and therefore collected from taxpayers – the government spending ratio starts to rise. The same applies when the health services – hospital surgery departments, for example – have access to increasingly effective – and costly – instruments and methods. By the same token, if child benefit is abolished and replaced by tax-free allowances, the government spending ratio falls, because the state takes in less in taxes and spends less. What this signifies for the families affected, whether it is more appropriate or more equitable, is a matter for debate. Does it make better sense simply by virtue of the fact that it reduces the government spending ratio? Of course, the government spending ratio could be lowered dramatically if pensions or health insurance were simply to be privatized. Whether pensioners today or in the future would feel more secure as a result is highly doubtful. So it is safe to assume that anyone disposed to conjure up the image of a state with too much financial power, based on a government spending ratio of between 40 and 50 per cent, is going to have ample opportunity to do so in the future, even if his local swimming bath or public library has to close for lack of funds.

For reasons that need not concern us in the present context, the tax and contribution ratio is always substantially lower than the government spending ratio. It covers what is paid by the public in taxes and social security contributions. In Germany it is nearly 10 per cent lower than the government spending ratio – so normally between 30 and 40 per cent. This is distinct from the tax ratio, which in Germany has fallen steadily over the past few years, despite the solidarity surcharge – which has not had any effect on the endless complaining about the tax burden.

The tax ratio has since fallen to 20.5 per cent (2004), and is below the OECD average. Anselm Görres, economist and former McKinsey consultant, explained in the *Süddeutsche Zeitung* of 25 August 2004 why he was not impressed by the whingeing, particularly from corporate tax payers: "Business taxes as a proportion of total tax revenues are very low in Germany, accounting for only 9 per cent of the total tax take. And they amount to only 3.3 per cent of GDP, which is barely half what most of our West European neighbors pay. When it comes to tax loopholes, we Germans are in a league of our own. For private investors in Germany, unlike most other market economies, increases in the value of their investments are completely tax-free. A Munich businessman once admitted to me quite openly: 'In actual fact my secretary pays more tax than I do.'"

So Germany is doing pretty well in the contest to attract inward investment by offering the lowest business taxes. Thirty years ago business taxes as a proportion of the total tax take were more than twice as high. This is why the man in the street continues to moan about high taxes, while finance ministers at the regional and national level, to say nothing of city treasurers, have the greatest difficulty in funding even the bare minimum of public services expected by our citizens.

It is neoliberal policy to demand tax cuts as a matter of principle. Where tax cuts have recently been made, they are never enough. When asked how government budgets are going to pay for these tax cuts, they airily intimate that this is not really their concern. Savings can surely be found from somewhere.

One argument often heard invokes the theory that led Ronald Reagan to push the national debt up to unprecedented heights. The theory claims that tax cuts speed up economic growth, which means that the state collects more in taxes at the end of the day. If the equation "lower taxes equal more taxes" were really correct, there would actually be no good reason why taxes should not be **progressively** cut virtually to zero. And any politician who did not cut taxes would simply be a fool. However, former German Finance Minister Hans Eichel learned otherwise. As we entered the year 2000 with the economy apparently in a very healthy state, he hoped to give a further boost to growth by cutting taxes as from 2001. But the opposite happened. And the subsequent stages of his reform program failed to get the economy moving again. His fiscal plans were in tatters.

Underlying the theory that tax cuts will lead to an increase in the tax take is the – generally unspoken – view that every euro that disappears into the public coffers is put on hold there and taken out of economic circulation. That these euros quickly find their way into other coffers, and that the state participates willy-nilly in the economy, is understood by the despairing tradesmen who have to lay off staff because the state no longer has any contracts for them. But neoliberal economists and politicians frequently behave as though they did not understand this.

There is probably no scientific formula that would allow us to calculate with certainty whether or not the tax cuts introduced by the Gerhard Schröder/Joschka Fischer government created more jobs than they destroyed. But we are surely entitled to ask the question. And if more money were made available to local communities, the economy as a whole would undoubtedly benefit.

Of course the falling tax yield also forces the government to dismantle unnecessary bureaucracy. But after many years of pressure on spending from the Ministry of Finance, there are not that many jobs left to cut. Now the lack of money is starting to bite in very different areas, as can be seen from a notice that appeared in the press at the start of 2005: "The prospects for professional musicians in Germany have deteriorated markedly in the last few years. More and more qualified musicians are failing to find permanent employment after graduation. In Germany there are currently 136 serious orchestras with 10,220 full-time posts. Since 1992 thirty-two orchestras have gone – either disbanded, amalgamated with others or even declared insolvent. Very few musicians find a new orchestra post when their old orchestra is disbanded, downsized or declared insolvent. For every vacancy advertised by the WDR Radio Symphony Orchestra in Cologne they receive up to 300 applications. Players in small and medium-sized orchestras earn between 1100 and 2900 euros a month before tax – and that is after playing in the orchestra for at least 16 years." (*Südwestpresse*, 4 November 2005)

We are talking about a relatively small group of people here. But they live in a country that for many centuries was proud of its highly developed and diverse musical culture – a culture with a strong provincial tradition as well. What a much poorer society managed to sustain, an incomparably richer society is no longer able to afford. And this incomparably richer society is surprised at the high level of unemployment.

VI. To see what practical neoliberalism looks like in its radical form, one must travel to the United States. In the late summer and early autumn of 2004 reports appeared in German news journals (*Die Zeit*, No. 36, *Der Spiegel*, No. 42) about an association that bears the harmless-sounding name "Americans for Tax Reform". Its chairman Grover Norquist not only has clear ideas about what the state should not be doing any more ("get out of education, get out of welfare, get out of healthcare"). He also wants to set one rate of income tax for everybody, the so-called "flat tax", ranging between 8 per cent and 10 per cent.

When one looks at the Bush administration's defense programs – to which Norquist does not object, incidentally – his proposals look like the daydreams of a nutcase. But Norquist is a successful political operator. He knows how to get the power that is necessary to implement such plans. Norquist persuaded all Republican senators and congressmen – with the exception of 21 renegades – to sign a pledge that they would never vote for a tax increase. This he calls the "oath". The oath is sworn in the presence of two witnesses, and remains binding until death. Bush and Cheney have both taken the pledge. Norquist keeps the names of the 21 *refuseniks* in his wallet, in the hope of being able to strike one off the list from time to time.

What distinguishes Norquist and his kind from German proponents of tax cuts is the brutality with which he sets out and pursues his goals. "My goal is to cut government in half in twenty-five years, to get it down to the size where we can drown it in the bathtub."

Or even more unequivocally: "Starve the beast!" The beast is the state, or more precisely the 50 states and their federal union, the United States. And Norquist is a politician, wielding a great deal of influence in the Republican Party. They are fighting for power in a state where the starving of the state is a recognized policy position within their party.

The fact that there are people in the US who want to starve their state should not surprise us. The fact that there are others who want to build up their country's military strength to make it the hegemonic power for the 21st century is merely the continuation of a long European tradition: think of Spain in the 16th century, France in the 17th, Great Britain in the 19th and Germany in the 20th century. But that there are quite a few Americans, and particularly in the Republican Party, who harbor both these aspirations at the same time – global hegemony and the starving of the state – may well cause Europeans to ponder. The former President George W. Bush, with a mandate from the people, did not only support, but in the eyes of many also embodied both these tendencies.

VII. Compared with Americans for Tax Reform, Germany's "Taxpayers' Alliance" looks like a harmless association of worthy businessmen intent on representing their collective interests as taxpayers vis-à-vis the state. They have hired a few trained economists (the Karl Bräuer Institute). They also seek – and find – publicity. None of which is cause for alarm or offence in a pluralist democracy. But if one takes a closer look at the methods of this Alliance, doubts about the worthiness of the enterprise begin to surface.

Just into the second half of each year, generally around the middle of July, the Alliance grabs the headlines by proclaiming "Taxpayer Remembrance Day". This is the day up until which – according to the calculations of the event organizers – the taxpayer has had to work for the state, as it were, and after which he is finally working for himself. The "tax-on-income ratio", generally in excess of 50 per cent, also includes social insurance contributions, of course, so that when we are said to be working for the state, we are in part working to provide for our own old age.

The figures published by the Bräuer Institute differ substantially from anything put out by serious agencies. In 2004 the Taxpayers' Alliance came up with the figure of 54 per cent for the tax-on-income ratio. The OECD figure was 40.8 per cent, while the Committee of Experts for Economic Development calculated 37 per cent.

But this need not worry the Taxpayers' Alliance, as long as most newspapers are content simply to reprint its figures without further comment, sometimes even concocting headlines from them. Figures given to the public by the German Minister of Finance, who heads up a professional ministerial bureaucracy, are closely scrutinized – and quite properly so. The figures put out by the president of the Alliance, Karl Heinz Däke, are almost invariably accepted without critical examination.

There were exceptions in 2004. On 16 July the *Süddeutsche Zeitung* took a critical look at the numbers game, published the day before. Journalist Michael Weisbrodt analyzed the method of calculation used by the Alliance, listed the various tricks employed and came to the conclusion: "Direct income tax in Germany has been lowered, but various indirect taxes have been increased. The Taxpayers' Alliance has complained constantly about the rising tax and contribution ratio. But the fact is, it has not increased – the yardstick has simply altered. End of story."

Another sweeping statement from the Alliance targets wasteful government spending. In 2004 the figure quoted was a massive 30 billion euros. But no evidence was supplied to support the claim. This was too much even for the *Financial Times Deutschland* (edition of 29 September 2004). It inquired where that figure had come from. The response was that the Federal Audit Office suspected that 5 – 10 per cent of tax revenues were wasted, which amounted to around 30 billion euros. The Audit Office immediately issued a denial. But like other figures from the Alliance, these 30 billion euros were reported without challenge in most German newspapers. And that is what counts.

The Alliance does outline some specific instances of what it sees as the squandering of taxpayers' money. But the sums involved are millions rather than billions – or in some cases just a few thousand euros.

For example, the city of Heilbronn, or more precisely the city's Department of Works, built an ice rink for 7.5 million euros. This was done when the Heilbronn ice hockey club was playing in the second division of the national league. But then the team was relegated. Now the Department of Works has to meet additional costs of 60,000 euros a year. How profligate of the Heilbronn city fathers, not to be able to foresee the relegation of their team and factor it into their calculations. Do we take it that the private sector is populated exclusively by clairvoyants, who know a year in advance whether the dollar is going to rise or fall, or whether the next summer is going to be hot or wet?

In the southern Palatinate region, near Ruppertsweiler, the controversial widening of the B 10 to create a 4-lane highway was finally approved subject to the condition that a footbridge is constructed to carry the European hiking trail, which crosses the road at this point. This bridge will cost 350,000 euros. Now the Taxpayers' Alliance is getting all worked up because walkers are not required to make the detour through an underpass "a few hundred meters" further on, since the authorities believe this would jeopardize their safety. One can argue about which is more important here: the quality of life and safety of the – evidently fairly numerous – walkers, or the notions of thrift cherished by the Taxpayers' Alliance. But to complain about a scandalous waste of money here – is not that a little shabby? Especially as anyone can now work out how long Mr. Däke would have to go without one of his three salaries in order to pay for the bridge.

The Taxpayers' Alliance will clearly stoop to anything in order to keep on hammering home its message to those who enable our country to function by paying their taxes honestly, for the most part: that this state of ours is nothing but a ravenous dragon, which swallows their money and then spits it out again somewhere else.

Here Grover Norquist of "Americans for Tax Reform" could only agree. Nor would he disagree with the conclusion that German newspaper readers are evidently supposed to draw from all this: that it is perfectly in order, morally justified, indeed required behavior, to resist the greedy monster and to deny it everything that can be saved from its clutches. But above all: that there is no need to be too particular about methods and means.

VIII. While it is true that the goals of the two organizations are not very far apart, and that the Germans have learned a thing or two from the Americans, there is nonetheless a deep divide between them in terms of style and language, in their awareness of power and their show of power. If Mr. Däke were to talk like Mr. Norquist, no serious broadcaster would ever invite him onto a discussion program. Clearly there are differences in the political culture here – or to be more precise, in our understanding of the state. And they are deeply rooted in our different historical pasts.

Nobody has thought more deeply about these issues in recent years than Gret Haller, the Swiss social democrat who – and this is a rarity in political writing – reflected on her own practice, in the shape of her work as the Ombudswoman for Human Rights in Sarajevo under the terms of the Dayton Agreement. She was constantly surprised by the fact that Europeans and Americans behaved so differently – and wondered why. Why they frequently wanted different things, why in the Dayton Agreement the Bosnian state is organized from top to bottom not as a polity peopled by its citizens, but as a balance struck between different ethnic groups. Back home in Berne, she immersed herself in reading and study. She wanted to know why the concept of the state means something different for Americans than it does for Europeans.

As a Swiss citizen she needed no lessons in federalism – how it works, its strengths and its hazards. The real issue here was the duties and responsibilities of the state. She published the results of her studies in a book that bears the somewhat misleading title *Die Grenzen der Solidarität. Europa und die USA im Umgang mit Staat, Nation und Religion* (Berlin 2002; cited here in the translation by Alan Nothnagle, *The Limits of Atlanticism. Perceptions of State, Nation and Religion in Europe and the United States*, Oxford/New York 2007).

In Sarajevo she had noticed "that the lack of a clear concept that I had been observing represented a concept in itself. The Americans often had no clear understanding of what a functioning state meant from a European perspective." (ibid., p.14)

She discovered that a "distrust of the state" (ibid., p.17) is an inherent part of American identity. And she found the explanation in Stephen Kalberg, an American sociologist: "The founders insisted that the state must be prevented from interfering with individual rights and societal developments; rather, it should ensure their unhindered unfolding by protecting free debate and the open exchange of views. The just and good society would evolve, early Americans were convinced, if the government avoided all attempts to guide the lives of citizens and to direct social and economic change."

If this is the legacy of the colonists, who after all emigrated in order to escape state paternalism, then politics in America and Europe are not the same thing. In Europe government legislation and politics are very much designed to influence the evolution of society. It is expected of a government and its parliamentary majority that they should at least set out to make society more just, more productive, more affluent and safer. Anyone seeking election has to state clearly where his priorities lie, where he wants to see more change, less change or no change at all. Even though 19th century conservatives were intent above all on preserving the status quo, they still consciously influenced society. In the 21st century, in an era when sustainable development can no longer be taken for granted, no government can afford not to try and influence the direction of change. On this point of principle all the democratic political parties in Germany are in agreement.

The government must give a direction to change. Energy supply, for example, cannot simply be left to the markets: it is also a matter for legislation, whether in the form of an eco-tax or financial incentives for renewable energy use. Is this the source of the conflict between Europe and the US over the Kyoto Protocol? The government, according to the European view, cannot and should not replace the market; but it must impose a framework that alters the impact of market events.

IX. To discover when American and European perceptions of the state began to diverge we need to go back to 1648, the year in which the Europeans concluded the Peace of Westphalia, ending 30 years of slaughter that began as a war of religion and was understood – and endured – as such by the people involved. In 1648 the modern state was inscribed in law, its sovereignty laid down both internally (the state monopoly on the use of force) and externally (*jus ad bellum*). Europe could only end the wars of religion by giving the state the right and the power to compel the warring religions to make peace.

The United States of America were established by people who had been obstructed, indeed prevented, in the practice of their religion by the state, and who were determined not to tolerate similar restrictions in the New World. So what emerged first in America was an extraordinarily vigorous civil society, which later went on to establish a state for the purpose of providing order and security. The state was also expected to guarantee total religious freedom. Consequently a "religion", in the US, is whatever claims to be one – even if Europeans shake their heads over it.

170 years ago, philosopher Alexis de Tocqueville described America's civil society with astonishment and admiration: "Americans of all ages, all conditions, and all dispositions constantly form associations. They have not only commercial and manufacturing companies, in which all take part, (…) The Americans make associations to give entertainments, to found seminaries, to build inns, to construct churches, to diffuse books, to send missionaries to the antipodes; in this manner they found hospitals, prisons, and schools. If it is proposed to inculcate some truth or to foster some feeling by the encouragement of a great example, they form a society. Wherever at the head of some new undertaking you see the government in France, or a man of rank in England, in the United States you will be sure to find an association." (Alexis de Tocqueville, *De la démocratie en Amérique*; cited here in the translation by Henry Reeve, *Democracy in America*, New York: D. Appleton and Company, 1899)

The American colonists were forced to rely on themselves. They got used to it. Their quality of life depended on themselves alone. Not that every individual literally "made his own way in the world". People worked together to achieve what was too much for one individual. But their expectations of the state, embodied initially by the British crown, then by the authorities in Boston or Philadelphia or even by the government in Washington, were very low indeed. Even their local officials were elected only for a few years at a time, to ensure that the power did not go to their heads. Civil society came first: the state came later. And everything of importance happened within civil society.

Why do the Americans refer to their government as the "administration", when it is manifestly more than just an administrative machine? Because originally "administration" was all they wanted, in the sense of a legal framework for the autonomous conduct of affairs within society. In Europe a clear distinction is drawn between the state and society, but not in America. When the Americans mean the state, they usually say "government". So what they call "non-governmental organizations" (NGOs) are known to the Europeans simply as "non-state organizations".

X. After their traumatic experiences with all-powerful states, many Europeans today are simply inclined to adopt the American perception of the state, the product of a very different but highly respectable history. Often they combine the skeptical American view of the state with sizeable expectations of their own government, in line with the European tradition. The government is expected to create jobs, bridge the gap between rich and poor, reduce the national debt, combat crime more effectively. But if it imposes a single tax increase, all the newspapers carry stories about the state having its hands in the citizen's pocket again. And a person who has his hands in someone else's pocket is a pickpocket. The state as pickpocket, and the government with all-round responsibility for everything: the two things do not add up.

So there is something to be said for Gret Haller's conclusion: that neoliberalism, with its devaluation of the state, is not a European but an American ideology, which for that reason too is apt to do less damage in the USA, with its strong civil society, than in Europe, where civil society did not predate the state, but evolved slowly in the shadow of a state that was for much of its history monarchic. Neoliberalism is certainly not indigenous only to America. It is economic liberalism taken to its logical conclusion, otherwise known as market radicalism. And yet the people of the southern hemisphere are not entirely wrong to see "Americanization" and a neoliberal-influenced globalization as two names for one and the same thing. The American public have viewed this form of globalization as a success for their own country, and even more for their own cause – whereas most Europeans have accepted it, rather, as an unavoidable fate, albeit with the determination to make the best of it.

Chapter 3

The Power of Globalization

I. Europeans struggle with the notion that the state, which in the 20th century sought – and abused – absolute power in more than one place, could waste away to the point where it is incapable of fulfilling even its simplest obligations. And they struggle even more with the realization that politicians and governments, who command the state's instruments of power, can do very little about it. We associate governments with power. We think of them as "having" power. And political morality is primarily a judgment on how they use power. Probably only those who have themselves toiled away at the political coal face are in a position to take the impotence of politicians seriously for what it is, or for what it has become, at any rate. So how do governments deal with their impotence?

By that I do not so much mean the countless different interests to which democratic governments always have to defer: the party grass roots, voters with their widely divergent interests, trade and industry associations, trade unions, the churches, auditing offices, parliamentary oversight exercised through the budgetary committee, various special committees, and not least the opposition and above all the media – serious and not so serious, electronic and print.

All this increases the risks, especially the risk of failure, catastrophic or otherwise. But what is worse is when the room for maneuver gets steadily narrower, when many things that a government or a minister regard as right, necessary and helpful are no longer possible, and when on top of that decisions are needed that they never actually wanted to take. There have always been situations where it was a matter of choosing the least of several evils. But globalization in its present guise imposes constraints of an entirely new kind.

And we are not talking here about the globalization of commodity markets. The fact that the export industry has to confront the challenge of global competition is not exactly news. European exporters have had to get used to this. The liberalization of markets has not only increased the number of competitors: it has also brought more buyers within reach, whether as consumers or investors. The export business has exploited its technical lead to offset the lower wages paid in other parts of the world. This is becoming more and more of a challenge, and Germany's position as the world's top exporting nation does not come with a lifetime guarantee. But this particular form of competitive pressure gets passed on to the trade unions rather than governments.

In 2004 the full force of that pressure was felt by the unions in Germany to a degree that was without precedent in the history of the Federal Republic. In order to prevent the export of jobs, the works committees at Opel, Siemens and Volkswagen had to agree to cut-backs and sacrifices on behalf of their fellow workers that went well beyond the reductions in employers' contributions against which they had vociferously protested not long beforehand. Suddenly the trade union leaders had to explain to their colleagues why they were just as helpless, and just as vulnerable to political pressure, as the government. At least the trade unions were able to point to naked threats, which governments generally cannot do, for two reasons: firstly, because nobody actually **says** "Unless corporation tax is halved, we will simply shift production to the Czech Republic", and secondly, because governments are always reluctant to admit their own impotence. What they say instead is that there is no alternative to their policy. Why there is no alternative generally remains unexplained.

What restricts the power of governments to act, and forces them to adopt a policy not anticipated in the manifesto of any major party, is the global movement of capital. It forces all states, regardless of who governs them, into a competition to attract inward investment. The threat to stop investing in a country is received by every government as notice of its own impending demise. Less investment or even no investment at all, means rapidly rising unemployment figures, which in turn signal election defeats.

It is not globalization that has made jobs scarce. The industrial revolution did that – and the rapid pace of technical innovation. Two hundred years ago most Europeans still worked in agriculture. Today it is only a small fraction of the population – and they produce more than all their hard-working great-grandparents. A hundred years ago the mining and textile industries employed millions of men and women. Today most of the pits have closed down, and textile mills have been converted into venues for rock bands.

So it has been clear for decades that most new jobs in the future are likely to come from the service sector. But where are people to find jobs when banks, building societies, insurance companies, the Post Office and the railways are constantly cutting staff, and when the telephone operator is no more than a dim memory of an antiquated technology? The economists and politicians who expected the "information society" to deliver hundreds of thousands of new jobs were simply being naïve. Of course there were new jobs: but the new technologies have destroyed more jobs than they created. It has, after all, been the object of technical progress for the past 250 years to make human labor unnecessary.

II. Because the industrial nations have been so successful in rationalizing work out of existence and increasing labor productivity as a result – as they have no doubt had to be for competitive reasons – politicians and sociologists began asking themselves in the 1980s where work still needed to be done in our societies, and sought to identify areas where additional work could enhance the quality of people's lives. And it had to be the kind of work that could not simply be rationalized out of existence by the latest technology.

They focused primarily on two areas, one of which was ecological restructuring, particularly in the energy industry. Renewable energy sources would be safer, more environmentally-friendly, more future-proof and at the same time more labor-intensive than energy from coal, oil or nuclear power. Much of what was envisaged back then has since been put in place by the Schröder/Fischer coalition government. The Law on Renewable Energy has led to the creation of new industries with thousands of jobs. It has channeled money in directions where opportunities could be seen for meaningful work that improved the quality of our lives. Political will has succeeded in getting a new market up and running. So clearly, such a thing is still possible in a globalized economy.

The second area that seemed to offer scope for job creation was interpersonal services – services that answered the individual's needs for health and well-being, education, personal contact, entertainment. The relevant professions ranged from pool attendant to nurse, from doctor to language teacher, from masseuse to doctor's receptionist, from home help to librarian, from concert violinist to curator of a local history museum, from occupational therapist to what many still referred to without guilt as "the cleaning lady".

Bright sociologists discovered that these services were more widely available elsewhere, largely through the private sector in the USA, publicly financed by the taxpayer in the Scandinavian countries, whereas in continental Europe, and in Germany in particular, neither private nor public provision was adequate, they said, for reasons that had to do with our welfare systems. So we had some catching-up to do. Whereupon people began to consider how additional service provision could be managed and funded.

But by the 1990s such thoughts had been swept aside. New jobs were to be created not by political strategies, but by the market – or to be more precise, by economic growth, which would be all the stronger the less the state intervened. That there could be such a thing as jobless growth was not disputed. Nor did anyone ever say where these new jobs were to come from. The most that was and is conceded is that even if growth rates are healthy, such jobs are hardly likely to appear in places where global competition is forcing companies to rationalize their production, i.e. in most areas of manufacturing, and now in many parts of the service industry too. Interpersonal services are being cut back due to a lack of money – and that from a level of service provision that is underdeveloped anyway by comparison with other countries.

III. Those who hope (and must hope) for salvation from economic growth – and they are by no means confined to neoliberals – must put all their faith in investments, or more accurately, investors. These investors impose terms and conditions – on trade unions, but above all on the state. They can do this in a globalized economy. They do it ruthlessly, and now they do it openly. If their conditions are not met, they threaten to take their money elsewhere. The power of blackmail that they wield is so obvious that for the most part they do not need to use it. As suitors, governments know what the objects of their affection expect, or are prepared to accept.

Before we rush to moral judgment, it should be pointed out that investors do not generally threaten out of arrogance or a desire to dominate. They too are under pressure. They have to deliver on "shareholder value". Their standing among their peers, and often their salary, depends on the share price. And they are under even greater pressure if the share price falls: if the company's stock market value is too low, it is vulnerable to takeover bids, more or less hostile, from competitors – who may come from the other side of the world.

Share prices are in competition with each other. Should a competitor's return on capital exceed one's own, even if the latter is high enough, this will affect the share price. Consequently modern businesses aim for, and achieve, much higher rates of return on capital than they did thirty years ago. So even if one's own return on capital has risen to an impressive 25 per cent, what happens when a competitor achieves 30 per cent?

Deutsche Bank made two announcements at the start of December 2004. The first was that its return on capital had risen to a healthy 18 per cent. The other was that it needed to cut 2000 jobs in Germany alone, because 18 per cent was not good enough: the bank was aiming for 25 per cent. The chief economics editor of the *Süddeutsche Zeitung*, Nikolaus Piper, did his touching best to make this comprehensible and palatable to a readership less well versed in economics (edition dated 3 December 2004). What Deutsche Bank was doing, he argued, would ultimately benefit employees too in the long run, because without profit growth there would be no jobs. The mantra used to be "no jobs without profits". Now it is "no jobs without profit growth". So the question is: how far and for how long must – can – profits continue to rise? As always, Piper argues his case persuasively. Major European banks – though he does not name them – are achieving returns of 27 per cent, and Deutsche Bank has to compete with them. How much profit is appropriate "is decided ultimately not by board chairmen, politicians or leader writers, but by the capital markets". And like it or not, these are global. Their decisions are taken without regard to people. Two months later it emerged that not everyone, not even on the editorial staff of the *Süddeutsche Zeitung*, was willing to accept this. Piper's colleague Ulrich

Schäfer wrote about the same story: "The strategy (of Deutsche Bank and its chairman, Josef Ackermann) is simplistic in terms of business economics and reprehensible in terms of social policy." (Edition dated 5/6 February 2005)

Is there a change afoot here? It was Germany's former Federal Chancellor Helmut Schmidt who sought to persuade people of the need for business to pursue profits, with the formula "The profits of today are the investments of tomorrow – and the jobs of the day after tomorrow". While it could have been objected, even back then, that by no means all profits are ploughed back in the form of new investments, the majority broadly accepted this formula as correct, or at least acquiesced in it. Will this majority now acquiesce in the new formula, which might go: "Because the profits of today are never enough, the job losses of tomorrow are the higher profits of the day after tomorrow"?

IV. The more deeply a non-economist – with some degree of political experience – studies the differences between the "Rhineland Capitalism" of the 1960s and 70s and the globalized, market-radical capitalism of today, the more it fascinates him to see how the real pressures of globalization and their neoliberal justification reinforce and complement each other, and how the two working together are driving and accelerating a process whose end-purpose and destination only theorists blind to reality think they know. Their selective vision simply ignores people as they actually are, the Europeans as they have been shaped by Christianity, the Enlightenment and democracy. Social justice may not mean anything to distinguished economists, but for the majority of Europeans it remains a yardstick for what happens in society, and for politics most certainly. Very few people are able or willing to define what justice is, but we all have a sixth sense for blatant injustice. When the board chairman of a company, who earns as much as 350 of his employees put together, announces 2000 redundancies in order to boost profits, it is bound to end in tears. Especially when it becomes known how much brainpower

Deutsche Bank and others expend – and hire in – in order to dream up all kinds of clever ways to avoid payment of the taxes due on their profits in Germany. Is the nexus between the constraints of globalization and neoliberal justification stronger, in the long run, than the hunger for justice?

In point of fact the global competition to attract inward investment does not constrain any national government to abandon political strategies for the labor market, especially that portion of the labor market which is not exposed to global competition. The fact that nearly all governments do so, that they seek salvation instead from economic growth alone, is probably due more to a mental constraint than to actual force of circumstances – namely the prevailing neoliberal climate of opinion which holds that the market can make everything happen, while governments can achieve very little, and certainly nothing of any use. So it is a matter of waiting to see what jobs the market throws up – or not, as the case may be.

But as soon as economic growth becomes the primary objective, governments can no longer afford to oppose the wishes of potential investors – who might become non-investors if they do. The competition to attract inward investment really hots up, and force of circumstance is reinforced by ideology.

The fact that the laws of "shareholder value" have pushed up the return on capital to unprecedented levels has a lot to do with the fear of being swallowed up by a more successful competitor, or in other words, with the constraints that capital operating on a global scale cannot escape. But by pre-emptively fending off all criticism, the neoliberal justification of this competition is effectively removing the brakes from a car that sooner or later – and sooner rather than later – is liable to come unstuck on a fast bend. How much longer will people go on accepting that a successful entrepreneur is one who increases the share value by sacking staff, while a successful government is one who cuts unemployment? Perhaps until they realize which one wields the real power here.

V. Professional protesters on the far Left were not the only ones who found it strange, improper and unjust that at the very time when the (slightly higher) unemployment benefit is being merged with the (lower) income support, the top rate of income tax, which for a long time stood at 53 per cent, was being reduced from 45 to 42 per cent. All kinds of plausible explanations have been put forward, of course: it is just a coincidence, the tax reform was planned much earlier, and anyway the changes will also benefit those on low incomes. Many have remained unconvinced. Would they have been convinced by the simple truth that the top rate of income tax needs to be "competitive" these days, pitched at a level where it does not trigger a flight of capital? Or by the painful truth that no finance minister in today's world can pull out of the race to lower taxes on business and high-earning taxpayers? And that no finance minister today can impose the taxes that he personally judges to be just and equitable? That would have laid bare the impotence of government, which is something that politicians of all parties shrink from.

Germany's Minister of Finance had promised immunity from prosecution to all those who had illegally transferred their money abroad, on condition that they moved it back by 31 December 2004. They would then pay just 25 per cent tax, and all would be well. Many jurists took the view that this arrangement violated principles of law. Neoliberal economists, on the other hand, doubted whether the investors could muster sufficient "trust in the state" – as if the state had somehow acted illegally and now had to work hard to win these people's trust. In any event, the proffered amnesty produced pitifully meager results. The vast majority of those who had escaped the taxman at home could not care less about the state's blessing, and left their money, doubtless with an untroubled conscience, where it could quietly earn the maximum interest. Which will not prevent them from laying the blame for Germany's spiraling national debt at the feet of incompetent governments.

The competition to offer the lowest business taxes operates under its own rules. Usually the process is set in motion and driven forward by smaller countries. Here significantly lower rates of business tax can quickly lead to a situation where the basis of assessment, namely the published profits – which in many cases have not even been made inside the country itself – grows to the point where it more than makes up for the lower tax rates. So small states like Ireland, Luxembourg, Austria and Switzerland – with up-and-coming countries like Slovakia now added to the list – can end up collecting more tax **after** a cut in the tax rate than they did before. Large countries do not have this option, because any inward investment has a proportionately lower impact on the basis of assessment: and they end up footing the bill. Which is why they also have an interest in reaching agreements on minimum tax rates. But such agreements are then blocked by the smaller countries.

Here again it can be seen how the pressures of competition and the prevailing climate of neoliberal thought become mutually reinforcing. When, of all people, the former Bavarian Premier Edmund Stoiber publicly supported minimum rates of business tax, at least within the European Union, he was given a pretty rough ride in the business pages of nearly every German newspaper. The business editors took the view that competition between countries was as healthy and productive as competition between companies. And lower taxes, they opined, are always a good thing. But then of course they are not responsible for funding the public sector. It is the same old story: those who refuse to accept the constraints fall foul of ideology. And this ideology always turns out to be much simpler and clearer in practice than it is in the textbooks. The interests that avail themselves of this ideology see to that.

VI. The conjunction of the pressures of globalization with market-radical ideology could soon claim another victim, in the shape of an institution that until recently was accepted without question

– namely progressive income tax, or in other words the principle that the proportion of income paid in tax increases with the level of earnings.

In Europe it was the liberals, not the social democrats, who pushed through the legislation to ensure that higher earners not only paid more tax, but also paid a higher percentage of their income in tax to the state than low earners. It was the Prussian national liberal Johannes von Miquel – who became the Prussian Minister of Finance following Bismarck's fall in 1890 – who introduced progressive income tax to Germany. As a long-standing member of the board of Germany's first major bank, who had emerged as the leader of the right wing of the national liberals, Miquel could hardly be accused of left-wing leanings. And neither the Minister of Finance after the First World War, Mathias Erzberger, nor the Minister of Finance after the Second World War, Fritz Schäffer, even thought about tinkering with the principle of progressive income tax. The only argument was about how steep the progression should be, and where it should end.

But all that is now a thing of the past. And the impetus for change comes from the East European countries – of all places – where the implosion of communism has been followed by the rule of gangsters. Many of the converted communists realized that if capitalism has won out over socialism, then the laws of capitalism must apply. These had been formulated by Milton Friedman. As early as 1962 he had put forward a proposal – admittedly for the eyes of the initiated only – for a "flat tax". In other words he was arguing for the abolition of progressive income tax and its replacement by one rate of tax for all.

What was an abstruse theory in 1962, even for then Germany's Federal Chancellor Ludwig Erhard, has now become the law in one East European country after another – not because globalized markets are forcing it upon them, but because the neoliberal advisers are recommending it, often with the entirely reasonable argument that a small country like Estonia, Serbia or Slovakia is able to suck in so much money and capital from larger countries that the state ends up by increasing its overall tax take. Consequently the flat tax has a built-in tendency to fall. In Estonia, for example, the tax rate is currently 21 per cent (down from 26 per cent), but the intention is to cut it to 18 per cent in 2011. In Lithuania the flat tax is currently 24 per cent (down from 27 per cent) and in Russia, where the mafia is sometimes more successful at extracting protection money than the tax office is at collecting taxes, the rate is a modest 13 per cent. In Serbia the flat tax is 14 per cent and in Romania it has stood at 16 per cent since the beginning of 2005.

It does not take a genius to work out what the consequences will be for the major industrial nations of Western Europe. It will be argued that the flight of capital forces us to follow suit. The various graduated tax models that are now being hawked around are no doubt designed primarily to wean us off our attachment to a progressive income tax. And in due course the simplest way to eradicate the minor injustices that occur at the transition from one tax band to another will be to introduce a flat rate of tax.

If progressive income tax is abolished, then it will ultimately be due to the influence of East European gangsters. It is their success in the post-communist countries that has placed the rest of Europe under these fiscal constraints. It will be interesting to see what happens when these constraints collide head-on with the consciousness of people in the great democracies of Europe. For what has been taken for granted for a century cannot just be swept away, and especially not with the argument that capital can leave the country, but the ordinary man in the street cannot. What counts, then, is not the neoliberal textbooks but their translation into practice, and the way this practice interacts with the real constraints of globalization.

In practice people are always in favor of less state, without saying where in theory the need for a properly functioning state begins and ends. In practice people are always in favor of deregulation, without reflecting that it is the job of the state to establish rules. In practice people are always in favor of privatization, without giving any hint as to where the limits of privatization might lie. In practice people are always in favor of tax cuts, even if they have just had one. In practice people always start by supporting a reduction in the top rate of tax, then a graduated tax model, and finally the introduction of one rate of tax for all. Above all: in practice the constraints that people point to have in large part been created by them.

What happens to the state in the process is of no interest to the neoliberal ideologues. That is not their responsibility. The state will get by somehow: it always does, after all. Let others worry about that if they want to. Well, it is high time somebody did.

VII. Does the European Union have to be – and remain – as helpless as the nation-states have become? Is the European Union not able – indeed called upon – to assume the responsibilities and functions that the nation-states have lost? Could it not close the loopholes, and call a halt to the endless race to cut taxes? No doubt it could: but it cannot right now – not yet, anyway. At the beginning of 2005 the then President of the European Council, the respected Prime Minister of Luxembourg, Jean-Claude Juncker, proposed a minimum level of corporation tax. But even he did not have any success. Why so?

Following in the footsteps of economist Jan Tinbergen, Fritz Scharpf distinguishes between negative and positive integration in his book *Regieren in Europa* (Frankfurt/Main, 1999). Negative integration means the abolition of customs duties, trade restrictions and all other obstacles to freedom of competition. So negative integration is essentially deregulation – in the case of the European Union, for the purpose of creating a large, free common market. The European Commission is responsible for overseeing this within the EU. It can act on its own authority, and if nation-states refuse to comply, it can appeal to the European Court of Justice, whose decision is binding.

Positive integration means new regulations for the whole of the EU that establish a framework for the market, transferring to the

European level responsibilities and functions that the nation-states have lost. Positive integration is all about re-regulation, in other words. Here responsibility rests not with the Commission, but with the European Council. And the Council's rulings must be unanimous – which they very rarely are in such matters.

So when questions are asked about the funding of Germany's regional state banks, and whether the provision of state guarantees distorts competition between European banks, the Commission is free to act on its own authority – because this is just a matter of abolishing something, namely a privilege peculiar to this group of banks. But when German politicians of nearly all parties call for a lower limit to be placed on business taxation, the Council gets involved – because this is about introducing a new regulation.

What this means in practice, according to Scharpf, is that the European Union has come a very long way on negative integration, but has made very little progress at all on positive integration. We can safely assume that this was the intention of those who decided on this distribution of powers. The Commission has kick-started the process of liberalization and selective privatization in many areas: telecommunications, aviation, airports, freight traffic, the energy market, even services that were previously subject to the Post Office monopoly.

So in many areas the Commission has curtailed the freedom of action of nation-states. But the ability of the Union to create its own, European freedom of action is limited by the fact that there are always one or two governments in the European Council – and it only takes one – whose interests diverge.

The result is that the Commission is able to intervene even in local government matters. It can advise local authorities to privatize the water supply, on the grounds that the price of water is subsidized by municipal waterworks, leading to an indirect distortion of competition: but nobody in Brussels is responsible for saying where these local authorities are going to get their taxes from. If the budget deficit of national, regional and local governments exceeds 3 per cent of GDP, the Commission has to step in. The fact that multinational companies are dodging payment of their taxes is not its concern. What this means, however, is that the European Union has so far taken away more responsibilities and functions from the nation-states than it was able – or willing – to assume for itself. Consequently the European Union has not strengthened but weakened the position of the state vis-à-vis business. In theory such a huge economic bloc ought to be capable of resisting the pressures of globalization, and the ruinous competition between nations to attract inward investment, far more effectively than any nation-state. In practice the distribution of powers in Brussels has tended to strengthen and sanction these pressures instead of alleviating them.

VIII. The fact remains: examples of positive integration, which is designed to claw back the power to influence policy-making lost by nation-states – and indeed more power than they lost in the first place – are very thin on the ground, whereas negative integration, aimed at removing barriers to competition across national borders, can move ahead at full speed.

This has to do in the first instance, of course, with the original goal of the European Common Market. The task undertaken by the Commission and the Brussels bureaucracy was to create a barrier-free market right across Europe. In the meantime the European Union has taken on very different functions – such as agreeing a common foreign policy. When and if enough people believe that the European Union is destined to show the way with a "European model" for the relationship between market, state and civil society, it should not be too difficult to devise a suitable legal framework. This will undoubtedly take longer than is good for the Europeans. But it is possible, if something like a European public emerges, if the Union becomes increasingly democratized, and if the majority of Europeans come to realize the extent to which their future is decided in Strasbourg and Brussels.

The European Union did not come into being as a result of globalization. It is the Europeans' answer to the madness of two world wars. The sovereign nation-state was long since past its prime by the time globalization became an issue. During the Cold War the two hegemonic powers, the US and the Soviet Union, had significantly curtailed the sovereignty of the European States, at least in foreign policy. Within its satellite states the Soviet Union also determined the broad shape of domestic policy – with the result that many people in these states now find it hard to give up their sovereign rights for the European Union, rights that they had won back only a few years previously, or, as in the case of Croatia or Slovakia, gained for the very first time.

After the Second World War the nation-states of Western Europe were at least able to shape their own social systems, their own fiscal policy, and – within limits – their own economic policy. Even if the US President was less than enthusiastic, they were free to nationalize their key industries, extend social provision to create a welfare state, and impose top rates of income tax on high earners that would be greeted with incredulous amazement today. But their freedom of action in the foreign policy sphere was limited, even in the case of France, which since the time of Charles de Gaulle had not allowed any US troops to be stationed on its soil, and which, although a member of NATO, refused to join its supranational organization.

The globalization of markets, particularly the capital market, has touched a more tender spot in the nation-state. If a country's foreign policy is determined by a foreign superpower, it is principally the officials working in the foreign service who notice. But if the state is starved of resources, everyone gets to feel it, especially the majority who live off their own labor and social welfare institutions. If a government quietly does the bidding of a powerful ally, it is a matter for discussion among insiders. But if a government's actions in the area of social policy are the opposite of what people expect, then it becomes a matter for discussion over the lunch table and around the water-fountain.

IX. Weakened though it is, the nation-state is still with us, and is likely to be around for a long time to come, not least in Europe. The European Union is not a state, and has no pretensions to be one.

Ulrich Beck has proposed the term "transnational state" to describe this weakened, dependent nation-state. (Ulrich Beck, *Was ist Globalisierung?*, Frankfurt/Main 1997; cited here in the translation by Patrick Camiller, *What is Globalization?*, Cambridge 2000) His immediate aim was to argue against those colleagues who were proclaiming the end of the nation-state, indeed the end of nations, of democracy, and even of politics itself. He countered with the argument: "The (national) state is not only antiquated but also indispensable", and this not only as a guarantor of basic rights or social welfare systems, but also "to give political shape and transnational regulation to the process of globalization" (ibid., p.108). For Beck, therefore, "transnational states" are not ailing institutions but "strong states", which derive new strength, the "power to shape politics", from "cooperative answers to globalization" (ibid., p.108). It is precisely in the cooperating national states that "a consciousness of compulsory cosmopolitan solidarity" can and must emerge (ibid., p.109). What drives these transnational states is no longer nationalism, but the "conscious realization of the necessity of transnational states" (ibid., p.109).

Beck's concept of the "transnational state" has not caught on. Perhaps it is too artificial, too intellectual. But that does not mean that the issue itself has gone away. One could also use a favorite word of Georg Wilhelm Friedrich Hegel to describe it: the German verb *aufheben*. As a professor in Berlin the philosopher from Stuttgart retained his Swabian turn of phrase, and for him *aufheben* means first and foremost "to preserve". But it can also mean "lift up, suspend" – and by extension from that, "cancel, invalidate". The nation-state, at least in its European guise, is not extinguished but suspended: preserved as an active part of the European Union, preserved for the duration within its present borders, with its present official language, its history, its cultural strengths and weaknesses, and for the foreseeable future with its social welfare systems too. But it is lifted up above national and nationalistic rivalries and prejudices, which led to the great wars of the past. At least war has been abolished between these states, and with it the *jus ad bellum*, or the legally sanctioned use of force, which has been part of the state since 1648. To that extent the traditional nation-state has ceased to exist: it has been suspended, annulled. In a later book Beck himself speaks of his transnational states as nation-states that are "not being dissolved but are instead being at once transcended and preserved (in the Hegelian sense of 'sublation')". (Ulrich Beck and Edward Grande, *Das kosmopolitische Europa*, Frankfurt/Main 2004; cited here in the translation by Ciaran Cronin, *Cosmopolitan Europe*, Cambridge 2007, p.72)

A key point in Beck's argument is the statement: "the model of the transnational state negates the national state but also affirms (the concept of) the state". (Ulrich Beck, *Was ist Globalisierung?*, Frankfurt/Main 1997; cited here in the translation by Patrick Camiller, *What is Globalization?*, Cambridge 2000, p.109) So Beck's transnational state is first and foremost a state – to which one might add: the same state, but one that is filled with new content, and that serves new functions alongside many of the old ones.

Which brings us, finally, to a question that we can no longer avoid: the question of what the state actually **is**, what the "idea of the state" is all about, and wherein the strength of a state lies.

Chapter 4

The Necessary State

I. The authority whom the first Christians in Rome were directed to obey by the Apostle Paul had a recognizable face: that of the Roman Emperor. Very few of his subjects between Gaul and Palestine had ever seen him in the flesh, but they all knew his name. His face was stamped on the coinage. Fifteen hundred years later, when Martin Luther forcefully reminded his followers of St. Paul's unequivocal injunction, especially in the aftermath of the Peasants' Revolt, the authority in question was nearly always a prince. He could expect, and demand, obedience, for his house had ruled the land since time immemorial, and furthermore he was prince by the grace of God. When he died – as die he must, like his subjects – his authority passed to his son. The word "state" does not appear in Luther's writings. It was first used in its modern sense by Machiavelli in the 16th century, in an Italy that was decades ahead of the rest of Europe.

The new term signaled first of all that here was something that was not synonymous with the ruling prince, something that existed in its own right, and made it possible for the monarch to exist, but which at the same time was conceivable in principle without him; something abstract but powerful, which encompassed an administrative apparatus, but was not subsumed by it. Following the Peace of Westphalia in 1648, the defining characteristic of the state was its sovereignty in the domestic and the foreign sphere, a sovereignty that extended to religious denominations, which it could compel to make peace. Sovereignty at home found expression in the state's monopoly on the use of force, and abroad in the *jus ad bellum*, or the right to wage war. This sovereignty remained in the hands of the princely ruler.

The first to take up the distinction between the monarch and his state and turn it to positive advantage was Frederick II of Prussia, when he called himself the first servant of his Prussian state. This conveyed the message that the state was even more important than the monarch. The state is not there for the monarch: the monarch is there for the state. This did not prevent him from trying to control every aspect of government in his kingdom. And it did not prevent his subjects from identifying this state with him, the king. But now the Prussian state was something that it was an honor to serve. Half a century earlier, Louis XIV of France had protested against this new-fangled separation of monarch and state with the famous dictum *L'état, c'est moi*: if the smart alecks among my subjects think they can or should talk about "the state" instead of – as is fitting – the King and his kingdom, the monarch and his subjects, then I must disappoint them. Like everything else, the state is none other than the work and the property of the King. If there has to be a state, then I am the state!

At that time there were also – as de Tocqueville later reminded us – regional and local authorities, aristocratic families, monasteries, towns, which did not owe their power to the king, and were not integrated into the state until later. For the peasantry certainly, whether in bondage or not, they were the ultimate authority, and often remained so into the 19th century.

Because the modern state, unlike the old ruling authority, has an abstract quality about it, it lacks a recognizable face. The Queen of the United Kingdom or of the Netherlands, the King of Spain or of Sweden, whose portrait still appears on the national coinage, are permitted and expected to represent their state, but they are not permitted to rule it. Those who do rule it, the prime ministers and premiers, stand not at the head of the state, but at the head of a group of state servants (ministers). It is open to anyone to criticize them, abuse them, and above all wish someone else in their place.

State presidents like those in Germany and Italy have a harder time of it than today's representative monarchs. By the time the Italians or Germans have got used to the face of their president, a new one is already being elected – and not by the people, but by the people's representatives. State presidents are generally overshadowed by their heads of government. If they succeed, at least for a short time, in becoming something like "the face of the Republic", then this is their own personal achievement. In France and the United States the representative head of state is also, like the prince in former times, head of the executive. He can become the face of the state for a period of office, even if only a bare majority voted for him. But he can also remain, for one half of the nation, the man who represents the other half only. So what can happen, even in venerable democracies like the US, is that the state acquires a recognizable face – but an ugly one.

II. If the state generally means something more concrete for the French than it does for the Germans, this has to do in part with the fact that Germany has a history of federalism while France has a centralist tradition. For the French, the state is very definitely the national state with Paris at its centre. For centuries Germany had no capital city, and until 1866 most southern Germans looked to Vienna as their point of reference rather than Berlin. The federal nation-state is more elusive and intangible than the centralized state. Its citizens find it easier to identify with the individual states (*Länder*) that make up the federation – Bavaria, say, or Saxony.

The towns and parishes, most of them older than the state, are part of the state, but are often not perceived as such. The mayor complains about "the state", and means the regional (*Land*) government, which has cut his subsidies. The regional government brings an action against the federal government in the Constitutional Court, the federal government is in dispute with the EU Commission. Where is the state in all this?

The state is divided up into several "layers", as the political scientists say. Martin Shaw even speaks of a "global layer". State functions and competencies are shared out between different agencies. Local authorities (towns and parishes) are responsible for the water supply and school buildings, while teachers and the police come under the jurisdiction of the *Land* or regional authorities. The federal government is responsible for social security provision, while customs duties fall within the remit of the European Union. Responsibility for an international monopoly on the use of force would rest with the UN. It is not easy to view all this as a single entity called "the state". Is it, in fact, too much to expect?

A federal state has many advantages. Self-governance at the municipal and parish level encourages democratic engagement within the local community. Local politics can be more exciting than regional politics. Many people follow local politics more closely than political events on the national stage. Germany's *Länder* can tap into loyalties that have evolved over many centuries.

But because the state remains an abstract concept in the federal system, it becomes an easier target for criticism. Anyone who wants to represent the state as a greedy monster does not need to specify whether he means the town, the *Land*, the national government or indeed the European Union. One can rail against abstractions until the cows come home.

Quite a few of our citizens – and especially the women – who only have disparaging things to say about the state, find their lady mayor marvelous, their town treasurer capable and efficient, the lady premier of the *Land* likeable, the police polite, the armed forces necessary and the foreign policy of the Federal Republic absolutely right. But what has all this got to do with "the state" as such?

Deeply rooted in history – and not just in Germany – federalism is suddenly modern again in other places, because it reflects the principle of subsidiarity. However, this salutary federalism also encourages sweeping criticism of the state. The principal beneficiaries of such criticism are those forces that see in the state an obstacle to free-market enterprise that cannot be small enough for them. That the local authority needs money to keep the open-air swimming pool open, and occasionally to buy a few new books for the public library, makes perfect sense to most people. If the regional government does not have enough money to pay a sufficient number of teachers, most people find this unacceptable. If Bavaria, of all places, has to cut 1200 jobs in the police force, many people find this worrying. And if the federal government has to postpone the repair and upgrading of a stretch of motorway for lack of funds, there is a storm of protest. But none of this alters the general view that the state is a pickpocket waiting to relieve us of our hard-earned cash the moment we relax our vigilance. Is the public good harder to discern, and easier to ignore, if the responsibility for it lies in a number of different hands? Or does this only hold true until such time as all the layers of state authority are so starved of resources that the public starts to feel the effects in their everyday lives?

III. There was a time when the paterfamilias could explain to his children in a few words what authority is, and who it is. But it is not possible to say what a state is in a couple of words. The term has to be defined by academics. The most precise definition to date, and therefore the one with the most international currency, comes from sociologist Max Weber. According to him, the state is "a human community that (successfully) claims the monopoly of the legitimate use of physical force within a given territory".

Contained within that formulation is what many others have said about the state: that a state requires a nation, a national territory and national sovereignty; that the state must possess a monopoly on the use of force and the means to assert it; that it needs to establish its legitimacy – in the past through the historically legitimized hereditary monarchy by the grace of God, and today through the free vote of the national electorate.

This implies that the state and the law are belong together. The state exists where laws are made, wrote the German-American theologian Paul Tillich. "The state upholds the law, and where the law is upheld, there the state is." (Renate Albrecht, *Paul Tillich Gesammelte Werke*, Vol. IX, Stuttgart 1956, p.124) Tillich elaborates on the meaning of the proposition that the state "upholds" the law: "Where there is no power to make and enforce laws, there is no state."

The law does not come out of nowhere, of course. It begins with the formalization in legal norms of what is customary. And what is customary is that the strong take for themselves the laws they need. This was well understood by Hermann Heller, the philosopher of law from Tillich's generation who died young. He wrote that it was "in the nature of the law and the state that they, like all things intellectual, owe their evolution to the struggle between competing social interests, but demonstrate their divine spark by the fact that they are constantly striving to free themselves from the embrace of competing interests." (Hermann Heller, "Gesellschaft und Staat", in: Herfried Münkler (ed.), *Lust an der Erkenntnis: Politisches Denken im 20. Jahrhundert*, Munich/Zurich 1994, p.210)

Or to put it more bluntly: it is not so easy to make might look like right. Injustice set down in black and white excites more opposition than injustice perpetrated in some village in the back of beyond. This is why Gustav Heinemann insisted that the primary function of the law was to protect the weak. The laws made, upheld and enforced by the state are there to protect all those who cannot protect themselves.

IV. In case such a definition should appear too abstract, here are a couple of contemporary examples by way of illustration. Where the state has lost its monopoly on the use of force, where warlords, mutinous mercenaries or plain criminal gangs rule by force – and that happens often enough today in Africa and Central Asia – the state has effectively ceased to exist. There is no state any more, so there is no law – and no protection for women, children, or the elderly against the Kalashnikovs wielded by marauding bands of soldiers.

Or, to put it in the context of the opening chapter of this book: Hitler's *Reich* was a state in the proper sense, whereas the Oceania of Big Brother depicted by Orwell was not. Where existing laws are manipulated, bent and broken, and where laws are passed that offend our sense of justice, there is still a state: not a state governed by the rule of law, but a state nonetheless. Where there are no laws and therefore no justice, there is no state. So not every organization that practices violence as a means of control can be called a state.

Osama Bin Laden's Al-Qaida, for example, is not a new kind of state, as Ignacio Ramonet claimed in the French news journal *Le Monde Diplomatique* in December 2001. According to Ramonet, there have been various kinds of state throughout history – the city-state, the region-state, the nation-state – and now globalization has brought us the *réseau-Etat*, or network state, that exists without territory and without written laws. The next thing to come along, he claims, will be the *entreprise-Etat*, or corporate state.

Stretching definitions in this way can only cause confusion. Bin Laden's trump card in the fight against conventional states is precisely the fact that he has no territory and no address, that he can therefore strike anywhere, but cannot himself be targeted or destroyed. What makes him powerful is precisely the fact that he is not restrained by domestic or international law, and that he, in contrast to every state on earth, can recruit and deploy suicide bombers. It is certainly true that Bin Laden knows how to exploit

67

successfully all the opportunities and methods of a globalized economy and globalized media. For this reason Al-Qaida could be thought of as a multinational enterprise dealing in violence. What Bin Laden has built up is a network of denationalized, privatized, commercialized, and therefore criminal violence. The fact that the President of the United States, a world power, has declared war on him has immeasurably enhanced his standing. But that does not make him a head of state. And neither does the piece published by American academic Philip Bobbitt in the *Financial Times* of 13/14 August 2002, where he argues along the same lines as Ramonet, albeit with the aim of justifying the "war on terrorism".

V. Then again, if the state today is being devalued and weakened not by those who once aligned themselves with Karl Marx in denouncing the state as the tool of the ruling capitalist class, but often by the very people who were identified with this "ruling class", this has to do with the fact that the law, as defined and laid down by the state, is always less accommodating and convenient for the powerful than the simple principle "might is right". Obviously one effect of deregulation is to get rid of antiquated or unnecessary rules devised by pedants. But if it is the task, and indeed the defining characteristic, of the state to establish binding rules, to regulate, to make and enforce laws, then those who regard deregulation as a good thing on principle will have it in for the state. Those, for example, who want to deregulate the system of protection against wrongful dismissal, are putting the rights of those who in this case are clearly in the stronger position ahead of the law laid down by the state, which has to weigh up the interests of both sides.

Or then again, when Federal Chancellor Helmut Schmidt described himself as the Chairman of the Board of Germany plc, it was undoubtedly an engaging gesture of modesty before all else. But it was also a rejection of any vestigial mysticism surrounding the idea of the state that some Germans, he suspected, still clung on to: and this was neither correct nor helpful. Quite simply, the state that makes, upholds and enforces the law is **not** a commercial enterprise. Even if the state has to keep a grip on its budget – or budgets, in the case of a federal state – its aim and purpose is not to make a profit, but to order the relationships between people by making laws and enforcing them. Consequently the state has the right to punish and imprison people who break its laws, whereas the manager of a company does not. To Helmut Schmidt's credit it should be said that he was well aware of this, and that when push came to shove he acted like a Chancellor and not like a business mogul. But those of less sound mind take his self-deprecation more seriously than he did himself. And that only leads to confusion.

Lothar Späth, who is an admirer of Schmidt, still finds it absurd, and certainly unjust, that he was hounded from office by the media of Baden-Württemberg because he flew around in business jets, averaging two flights a week. As Premier of Baden-Württemberg he had only been doing his duty, of course: helping the economy and therefore businesses in the region. Why should they not pay for the privilege? Späth was right in so far as his critics never said why they thought this was scandalous. Had the state been a service enterprise for the promotion of economic growth and Späth the board chairman of Baden-Württemberg plc, then he would have done nothing wrong. On the contrary, he would have been a model CEO. But he was the first representative of a state: and as such he must avoid any appearance of being beholden to private companies.

Späth's critics should have taken the trouble to clarify their own position on the state, from which they attacked the wily politician. Späth resigned: but there was no debate about what a state is, and what it must require from its servants.

VI. As a close ally of the neoconservatives who has hitherto been a fervent champion of the market, Francis Fukuyama now argues the case not just for the state, but for the "strong state". But what is that? The professor of international political economy seeks to establish a distinction between two forms of "stateness": the range of functions and competencies ("state scope") on the one hand, the ability to enforce law and implement policy ("state strength") on the other. State scope encompasses the welfare state, state intervention in the economy or even state control of the economy. For Fukuyama this range of tasks constitutes at best an imaginary strength. The real and desirable strength "includes (…) the ability to formulate and carry out policies and enact laws; to administrate efficiently and with a minimum of bureaucracy; to control graft, corruption, and bribery; to maintain a high level of transparency and accountability in government institutions; and, most important, to *enforce* laws". (Francis Fukuyama, *State-Building: Governance and World Order in the 21st Century*, New York 2004, pp.8-9)

He divides states into four groups. In first place come states with small scope but a lot of power to get things done – and here he is thinking in the first instance of the USA, of course – while at the bottom of the list are states that set out to do a great deal but achieve very little, or in other words states that attempt – vainly – to combine broad scope with insufficient power to enforce. The examples he cites, rightly or wrongly, are Brazil and Turkey. He knows, of course, that there are also states with broad scope **and** significant power to enforce. As an example of this second group he cites France. In group three are the completely impotent states, which seek to do little and achieve less – or in other words, which combine small scope with even less power to enforce. He cites Sierra Leone as an example – a land bedeviled by civil war.

The distinction between what a state sets out to do, what it takes on, and what it actually achieves and gets done, is a useful one in itself. The criteria proposed by Fukuyama are applicable to all states, not just third-world countries. And his argument consciously acknowledges Max Weber's definition of the state. The state only exists where a monopoly on the use of force can be both legitimized **and** enforced. The question to which he, as an economist, gives little thought is the relationship between scope and the power to enforce.

This can be seen, for example, in the way he characterizes the US state – with whose history he is better acquainted than his European critics – as a "strong" state, while being fully aware of the Americans' skeptical view of the state and how that view has shaped American institutions. "The essence of stateness is, in other words, enforcement: the ultimate ability to send someone with a uniform and a gun to force people to comply with the state's laws. In this respect, the American state is extraordinarily strong: it has a plethora of enforcement agencies at federal, state and local levels to enforce everything from traffic rules to commercial law to fundamental breaches of the Bill of Rights." (ibid., p.6)

VII. So is it merely mischievous to ask whether – therefore – a state becomes stronger the more of its citizens it puts behind bars? If so, then the American state would be many times stronger than the states that make up the European Union. Is California particularly strong, on the grounds that it spends as much money on the penal system as it spends on higher education? Is it just coincidence, and of no relevance, that expenditure on the penal system has grown in inverse proportion to the decline in expenditure on social security? Or more fundamentally: can the power of a state to enforce the law be entirely unrelated to the services it provides for its citizens, to the tasks that it undertakes? And if the answer is "no": is the relationship between the two everywhere the same?

It is not appropriate for a European observer to lecture the Americans on what is possible or right in their country. But it is reasonable to ask questions. What does it say about the state monopoly on the use of force in the US that there are now three times as many employees of private security firms as there are policemen? If this trend continues – and it is continuing – when will the US reach the point where protection against crime becomes a commodity, a commodity which, like other commodities, some people can afford and others, many others, cannot? Can a state – if we accept Max Weber's definition – allow this to happen? What does it say about the strength of the state when millions of families retreat into so-called gated communities, hiding away behind walls and fences, while they pay to be protected by privately hired security personnel?

And what does it say about the strength of the state when the police will only venture into the slums or no-go areas of the larger cities by day or in force, while criminal gangs run the show the rest of the time? Or more generally: can one still speak of a "strong state" when the monopoly on the use of force is being eroded from below and above, so that it is only relevant any more for a – dwindling – majority in the middle?

How the United States answers such questions is its own affair. All that a European can say is this: certainly not by failing to recognize the privatization of violence as a problem and blithely pressing ahead with it. And certainly not by declaring war on privatized violence around the world, while promoting it at home.

VIII. More important is another question, which Fukuyama does not, and doubtless cannot, ask: would it be possible in Europe, in France, Sweden or Germany, to drastically reduce the scope of the state – its responsibility for social welfare, for example – without diminishing or jeopardizing its power to implement policy, its ability to enforce the law? In short: is the minimal state, which neoliberal economists think is good for us, actually viable?

Is what neoliberal economists regard as the ideal state compatible with what Europeans – and perhaps not only Europeans – expect from their state? Are we not overestimating and overtaxing the economists by letting them tell us what the "right" state is? Do they have the necessary expertise?

Economists can tell us what the economy needs, and what it does not need. They cannot tell us what people need, even less what they want – and certainly not what they should want.

Perhaps we would be better off with the political scientists and sociologists after all. They have now begun to look again at the state and its functions. In Bremen four academics from three different institutions – Michael Zürn, Stephan Leibfried, Bernhard Zangl and Bernhard Peters – have got together to form the "Collaborative Research Center 597", with the avowed aim of studying "statehood in transformation". Their point of departure is the "Western-style democratic constitutional interventionist state", which they refer to, as is now fashionable, by its acronym "DCIS". The DCIS combines "four central dimensions of modern statehood":

1. The monopolization of the means of force and of tax collection within a specific territory has resulted in the modern "territorial state".
2. The recognition that the state is internally bound by its laws and may not intervene externally in the laws of other states has made possible the sovereign "constitutional state".
3. The formation of a common national identity – the people within the territory of a state consider themselves a community, and this is linked to the claim for political self-determination – has led to the "democratic nation-state".
4. The recognition of the goal to increase the wealth of society as quickly as possible and to distribute it fairly has led to the development of a "social interventionist state".

The important point is made that although these four "dimensions" can be analyzed as separate entities, they are in fact interdependent and mutually complementary. The interventionist state without the constitutional state would lead inevitably to the abuse of state power, the constitutional state without social intervention would forfeit consent, and both would collapse rapidly without the monopoly on the use of force held by the territorial state. And the democratic nation-state cannot simply be dissolved without harming the constitutional state. Suspended perhaps, but not dissolved.

This democratic constitutional interventionist state owes its legitimacy to the *demos*, the people, the men and women – *citoyens* and *citoyennes* – who make up the state, endorse it and support it. It is dependent on their loyalty. This is what sustains it – not just the once, when the constitution is voted into place, but constantly and always. Certainly, a properly elected democratic government can survive a great deal, especially as the electorate can vote it out of office. But can a democratic state survive if the majority of voters come to the conclusion that it does not matter who one votes for, since the real decisions are made elsewhere, by people who have not been elected?

Democracy without democrats does not last long, as the Germans have discovered to their cost. While it can be extended into society and implanted more deeply there, democracy is primarily a type of state and a system of government. To function properly it needs power, the power of those to whom the people have transferred their power for a season through the electoral system. This power, like all other forms of power, needs to be monitored vigilantly. But it has to be visible in the practical capacity of our rulers to decide issues one way or the other.

IX. The non-economist is well advised to leave the argument about the economic function of the welfare state to the experts. But he is entitled to ask questions. What good would it do an industry that complains about the under-use of its production capacity if pensioner Joan Smith could not afford a new vacuum cleaner, television, or warm shoes for the winter? How would it help our farmers if Mrs. Smith started eating cheap margarine instead of butter? And how would it help newspaper publishers if Mrs. Smith were forced to cancel her local paper? More generally: what would the abolition of the welfare state mean for an economy that is able and willing to produce and sell more, not less?

Whether the welfare state should be included within the proper "scope" of the state or excluded from it is a question best not put to economists in the first place. The real question is rather this: are most European democracies politically stable despite the fact that they are welfare states – or because they are welfare states? How stable would a democratic state in Europe be if it announced that it was not responsible for matters of social security? We do not need more scientific studies: the answer is obvious to anyone who has observed how large sections of society in France, Italy, Germany or Austria have fought against even modest cutbacks in the social services budget, against the raising of the retirement age, and against the introduction of stricter qualifying rules for welfare recipients. The vast majority of Europeans expect their state to assume responsibility for their social welfare in old age, if they are incapacitated by ill health or injury, and especially if they are unemployed. They are prepared to assist the state by paying the necessary contributions, but would have nothing but contempt for a state that would allow its citizens to fall through the net at a time of crisis, whether personal or socio-economic. Such a state would have forfeited their loyalty. For Europeans, the different "dimensions of statehood" are all parts of one whole.

Whether this is to be regretted or welcomed is irrelevant. This is the way it is. And it is deeply rooted in European history. The creator of Germany's social security system, *Reichskanzler* Bismarck, was a highly conservative man. And of course he was motivated in part by tactical considerations, the need to hold back the rising tide of social democracy. But he had also read his Bible, the Old and New Testaments, and he was familiar with the tradition of German cities, whose hospices took in the infirm and the sick back in the Middle Ages. Here in Europe, the idea that the state has a social responsibility was not invented by socialists, and certainly not by Marxists, but by Christians.

X. We have photographic evidence to show that the men and women who labored from 1948 to 1949 to draft the Basic Law of the new Federal Republic of Germany were pretty emaciated figures: gaunt faces, skinny frames clad in clothes that were many sizes too big for them. They knew the meaning of hunger. The famine conditions of 1947 were still fresh in their memories. They all wanted to rebuild the shattered country and its economy as quickly as possible. But it did not occur to any of them to preface the new constitution with the sentence: "The aim and purpose of this Republic is the pursuit of economic growth." Instead they decided to begin with the simple declaration: "The dignity of man is inviolable." They had all learned, of course, that the dignity of man can very easily be violated, injured, defiled and mocked, but not destroyed as a result. Which is why the next sentence is so important: "To respect it and protect it is the duty of the state and all its powers." Anyone can invoke this declaration in a court of law. It is enshrined in German law. Of course, it was formulated as a response to what had happened in the German state, and through the German state, just a few years earlier. Now it was to be the paramount duty of the state to prevent the same thing from happening again. And all things considered, it has done a pretty good job so far.

There is a thread that connects this first Article of Germany's Basic Law with the twentieth, which states: "The Federal Republic is a democratic and social federal state."

An institution charged with respecting and protecting the dignity of man cannot excuse itself from social responsibility. Article 20 does not say, of course, how this responsibility is to be discharged: what it does say is that whoever would protect human dignity must also ensure that people do not descend into a poverty that is contrary to all human dignity. In rich countries especially, poverty is seen as degrading. That was how Federal Chancellor Konrad Adenauer understood the Basic Law, too. He it was, after all, who pushed through the index-linking of pensions and equal representation in the workplace.

How the social responsibility of the state is to be discharged is a matter for renegotiation by parliamentary majorities in each new age. A good few European states have restructured their social welfare systems, or are in the process of doing so. They can of course consult any number of academic studies on the subject. One of the most useful is Gøsta Esping-Andersen's *Why we need a new Welfare State* (Oxford, 2002). The author describes a reforming tendency that is now universal: "Mechanisms in the current social security system that discourage people from being active should be discarded as much as possible." (ibid., p.X) But encouraging people to take responsibility for themselves also requires "full solidarity with those who have become victims through circumstances beyond their control." (ibid., p.XIV)

In practice social responsibility means different things at different times. But the fact that the state **has** such a responsibility is not only enshrined in the constitution. It is firmly anchored in human consciousness. Which means: the notion that curtailing the "scope" of the state will augment its power of enforcement in core function areas – such as the monopoly on the use of force – ignores the reality, or at least the European reality. The opposite is likely to happen. The ability of the state to uphold law and order – the primary function of the state, and not only for Fukuyama – would not be enhanced by such a move, but put at risk. Law and order, or in other words obedience to the law, is only possible in a democratic community if the citizens of this state acknowledge it as their own. If the four dimensions of statehood cease to be mutually complementary, the state starts to become unstable.

The strong democratic state is the state that is willed by its citizens as a protective cloak for society, shaped with the help of their critical engagement, and adequately funded by their taxes. The welfare state is an integral part of such a state. The idea cherished by some economists – that it is possible to strip the state of everything that they consider superfluous, while leaving some notional essential core intact and fully functional – is pretty naïve. Or to put it more plainly still: the democratic constitutional state is not an option without the welfare state – not in Europe, at any rate.

Chapter 5

Limits to Privatization

I. In 2001, as Francis Fukuyama tells us, Milton Friedman engaged in a self-critique. A decade earlier, he said, he had had only three words of advice for countries that had escaped the communist yoke: "Privatize! Privatize! Privatize!" But he conceded that he had been wrong. "It turned out that the rule of law is probably more important than privatization." As usual in history, the author of the doctrine is more flexible, more generous-spirited and less self-opinionated than his followers. As a great economist, of course, Friedman does not ponder the political question of whether the rule of law can exist in isolation, and what kind of state is necessary for the rule of law to function properly. But he does open the door to a less ideological debate about privatization.

The subject was already ideologically charged before Friedman was born. Ever since the socialists believed that salvation lay in the "socialization of the means of production", they encountered resistance from those who saw in it something else: an end to economic progress, if not the end of freedom. The socialists were for property held in common, the others were for private property. Their argument was about fundamental principles, and the tide has swept back and forth. Following the world economic crisis of the early 1930s and the Second World War – the outbreak of the latter certainly not unrelated to the former – a wave of nationalization swept over Europe. Very few of its champions argued their case on purely economic grounds. It was not that the economy would run better if the big banks or the steel industry were in state hands, thought the socialists in France or Britain, but that this would make it more difficult to convert economic power into political power.

Since the 1980s the tide has washed back the other way. Hardly anyone talks any more about economic power and its conversion into political power. Now people privatize because private enterprise is thought to be more effective, more likely to stimulate growth. The wave of privatizations gathered further momentum after the fall of communism. People started privatizing everything in sight, often for the simple reason that it was the fashionable, modern thing to do.

The ideological battle lines did not disappear altogether, but they became blurred. Even the democratic Left played along, with greater or lesser conviction, whether because budgetary constraints were more persuasive than principled reservations, or whether because politicians do not like to buck the mainstream, particularly when it is enshrined in directives from the EU Commission.

Among those who observed this flood wave of privatizations from the outside, with more or less scientific detachment, the ideological battle lines were generally more easily discernible than in day-to-day politics. So it is that today we have plenty of studies that either celebrate privatizations as progress, or else condemn them as reactionary machinations.

II. It was a good idea when the think tank Club of Rome decided to establish a working party to look at privatizations around the world, to find out what advantages or disadvantages they had brought for the economies – and more especially for the populations – of the countries concerned, and in what ways they had made life easier or more difficult. What emerged is a 400-page study with a title that recalls the Club's first and most celebrated publication. In 1972 it had been the *Limits to Growth* that had given the world food for thought: in 2005 it could well be the *Limits to Privatization*. And in case anybody should accuse the editors and co-authors of the report, Ernst Ulrich von Weizsäcker, Oran R. Young and Matthias Finger, of ideological bias, the study is subtitled: *How to Avoid too Much of a Good Thing* (London 2005).

The book looks at privatizations in all areas of the economy, from mining to telecommunications, from electric power to cultural heritage, from railways to water supply, from the police to the prison service. Examples of successful and unsuccessful privatizations are discussed. More importantly, the authors examine the specific reasons why something was successful or not, or in some cases why it started well, but then went wrong.

It is intriguing for a German reader to learn why the privatization of the railways was a success in Japan, but in Great Britain was such a total flop that the state had to progressively take back control of the railway system. The interesting question is where does the German railway *Deutsche Bahn* fit into the scheme of things: is it more like the Japanese model, or closer to the British one? Certainly a lot of the things that annoy and enrage the British public can also be found in Germany: trains simply being canceled, because there is no back-up locomotive available in the event of a breakdown, or passengers on an ICE queuing for the one functioning toilet on the train, because the job of repairing toilets is not effectively managed. In any event, *Deutsche Bahn* has already adequately demonstrated that poor business decisions are not the exclusive prerogative of state-owned enterprises.

Increased competition is generally acknowledged to be one of the main aims of privatization. And where this is achieved on a lasting basis, customers can benefit from better and cheaper services. But it is a different story where a public monopoly is

81

simply replaced by a private one. This applies principally in areas where there are "natural monopolies", or in other words, where competition is hardly possible. It simply makes no sense to lay two or three water supply pipes next to each other in the ground. And where several bus companies try to compete on the same routes in a small provincial town, none of them ends up making money. So the result is a natural monopoly.

Whether one of the few internationally active water companies can use its natural monopoly in the same way that private monopolies are used – and abused – depends on the specific terms and conditions negotiated at privatization and fixed by contract.

III. From Bolivia, one of the poorest countries in Latin America, come reports of two contrasting experiences. One was in Cochabamba, where the Bechtel Corporation pulled out hastily when demonstrations against higher water charges threatened to turn nasty. The other occurred in the capital La Paz, where the municipal authorities, together with private enterprise, had learned some lessons from the disastrous Cochabamba affair. Water from the Andes had been brought to La Paz – which stands 4000 meters above sea level – back in the late 1960s, with German development aid. In 1997 the World Bank called for the system to be privatized, because the municipal supply company Sampana was unable to keep pace with the city's growth. A French-Argentinian-Bolivian joint-venture company (AISA) was granted a concession for 30 years. The French-dominated AISA invested in water extraction and sewage disposal, increased the number of connections by 45 per cent over five years, and concentrated particularly on supplying the rapidly expanding suburb of El Alto. Water charges were frozen for the first five years, then rose by 38 per cent. But as the standing charge, which had affected low-volume water users the most, was abolished at the same time, even the poor were able to live with the increase.

The usual conflicts have arisen, of course, between the municipal authorities and private interests in La Paz, particularly when the water charges were up for renegotiation in 2002. But on balance privatization has brought more advantages than disadvantages for the population of La Paz. How things will look when the 30-year concession runs out, is another question. The latest news from La Paz and El Alto is not encouraging.

From these two contrasting stories from the same country, Bolivia, the Club of Rome study concludes that it is necessary "to think on a case-by-case basis". But at the same time it formulates general principles that apply not only where a natural monopoly leads on to an economic one:

1. A private water supply can be both effective and socially responsible "if the incentives for the investor are set intelligently and from the very beginning, including the tender".
2. Even the smallest details in the terms and conditions of the contract affect the outcome. "They must be considered and phrased far more carefully than has often been the case elsewhere, with predictably disastrous results."
3. If the specific terms of the contract are properly drafted – with outside advice if necessary – in the interests of the community, leaving no room for interpretation, then even a small town can get involved with big corporations without the poor necessarily having to suffer in consequence. (Ernst Ulrich von Weizsäcker, Oran R. Young and Matthias Finger, *Limits to Privatization. How to Avoid too Much of a Good Thing*, London 2005, p.21)

IV. So the investigation into the Bolivian examples of water privatization comes to the same conclusion that applies more generally: any success stories presuppose "a strong state capable of defining and, when necessary, policing the rules of the game". In other words, a weak state that cannot mobilize the necessary legal expertise to square up to the multinational corporations, a state that is unable to enforce the terms of the contract, should leave privatization well alone. Privatization and deregulation together – and the pairing of the two forms part of the credo of the neoliberals – have "predictably disastrous results". Privatization needs more regulation, not less. Where such regulation fails, where the private partner refuses to accept it, it is better not to privatize.

Anyone who has ever sat on a municipal council, or at least followed local politics closely, will immediately recognize the scenario. When the refuse collection service, a bus route or the municipal gas supply is being privatized, every effort must be made to anticipate and contractualize all the things that the local council has hitherto decided. In the past the council had to take account of the wishes of housewives who did not want their dustbins overflowing, or of local residents who wanted a bus service to their isolated hamlet. And if local councilors ignored such wishes, their chances of re-election were jeopardized.

Once a service has been privatized, local politicians no longer have any say in the decisions. But in the eyes of local residents they remain responsible. So they must do their utmost to ensure that the interests of their constituents are underwritten for many years to come, in the full knowledge that they can never succeed entirely.

Conflicts of interest between economic viability and the public good, which come up from time to time in every council chamber, have to be resolved in advance for decades to come. This is a challenge that can prove too much even for the best lawyers. So when public services were privatized regardless as if there was no tomorrow, there must have been good or compelling reasons why. The study identifies three principal reasons. The first is a careful calculation of what is likely to be cheaper for the consumer in the long run. Not without reason, people are often driven by the pressure to innovate, and consequently to invest. Those who face competition have good reason "to turn to the most modern technologies available". (ibid., p.153) This normally involves redundancies, because modernization saves labor. All the same, innovation can benefit the customer, whether in the form of lower prices or through greater product reliability. It can also, as in the case of the telecoms industry, open up entirely new possibilities. Interestingly, the study notes that many firms are now cutting their R&D expenditure, forced to retrench by "cut-throat competition on the global markets". (ibid., p.153)

The second reason – not a good one, but often a compelling one – is the pressure on the public purse at the state or local level. This argument carries conviction even if it is by no means clear that the consumer will benefit from privatization at the end of the day. To privatize responsibly, one must be in a good negotiating position. When people privatize out of necessity, because the city – or state – is getting too deeply into debt, so that they are effectively being forced to sell rather than privatize, they are negotiating from a position of weakness. They really should not do it: but they have no choice. Only someone who is intent on using privatization to weaken the enfeebled state still further can feel comfortable about such a transaction.

The third reason is fashion. It is – or was – a sign of modernity, proof that one had read the signs of the times, when the city's department of works was privatized.

Since this unconvincing reason frequently went hand in hand with a belief in the salutary power of deregulation, it is not surprising that the only positive outcomes noted in the study almost all relate to privatizations based on thorough scrutiny, detailed calculations, careful formulation and regulation.

V. How one judges the record depends of course on the criteria one chooses to apply. Someone who is only concerned with the economic benefits will judge differently from someone who also takes into account the political consequences, particularly at the local level. It is even possible to see the same outcome as a success or a failure, depending on one's point of view.

This is the case with what the study calls "cross-subsidies". (ibid., p.355) In many European cities the department of works has used the surpluses accruing from the sale of electricity or water to subsidize a loss-making local public transport system – generally bus routes – in order to hold down fares to an affordable level. Once the various municipal services have been privatized, this is no longer possible. The study finds that this is to the disadvantage of the people who need electricity, water – and a decent bus service. The neoliberal economist will argue that privatization simply removes a subsidy that has been distorting the market. The fact is that the money that once went to subsidize local public transport is now channeled into the pockets of private shareholders. And for that the bus passenger pays more, whether she/he can afford to or not.

Furthermore, the argument about distortion of competition does not cut much ice here. A person living in Munich cannot opt to use the Stuttgart tram service instead – even if it is cheaper than its Munich counterpart.

Not everything that reduces costs in the wake of privatization is necessarily the result of better management. All too often, says the study, people are hired without proper qualifications, particularly in the case of private schools, prisons or private police forces. And that leads to "tremendous negative effects for the quality of services".

Sometimes, too, costs and charges increase after privatization. A case in point is the German system of fire insurance for buildings. For many years this compulsory insurance was provided by a state-run institution. It had a monopoly. Its surpluses were used to subsidize fire services. Now, when private insurance companies compete for business at great expense, homeowners foot their advertising bills through higher premiums, while the shareholders get the money that previously went to the fire services. Which is more important: the common good, or the pure doctrine?

What the Club of Rome study does not address is the question of whether entrepreneurial abilities are confined to the private sector, or whether they can be successfully employed in state or municipal enterprises. The regional government of Baden-

Württemberg, for example, steadfastly refuses to relinquish control of the former monastery brewery Rothaus in the southern Black Forest, which was taken over by the state of Baden 200 years ago. One of the reasons is that the profits made by this enterprise help to fund the public purse. Would Rothaus beer be improved by privatization? Would they sell any more of it?

In the town of Schwäbisch Hall (population 36,000), the department of works is a limited company wholly owned by the town, and it initiates activities that extend far beyond the town itself. Not only does it generate some of its own electricity from hydroelectric power, wind power, combined heat and power plants and photovoltaics, but it also trades in energy, sells energy services, and owns a stake in the departments of works in other cities, such as Sindelfingen, home of Daimler-Benz. It even supplies heat and power from a cogeneration plant to a large hospital in St. Augustin, in the distant Rhineland region.

The chief executive of the department makes full use of the opportunities created by the liberalization of the energy market, while at the same time accomplishing much of what the city council and mayor want to see done in the way of promoting a sustainable energy supply for the future. And on top of this, he ensures that the municipal baths, which are now owned by the department of works, do not have to close despite substantial deficits. The confidence that the local residents have in their department of works was demonstrated when the latter issued a bond to fund renewable energy – which quickly brought in twice the amount of money it needed. So it **is** possible to combine economic success, the common good and sustainability without privatization.

Word has got around that Schwäbisch Hall, with its department of works in town ownership, has done better than the town of Gmünd 50 km further south, which sold off its department of works. Local politicians regard it as quite something that the town councilors who sit on the supervisory board of Schwäbisch Hall's department of works are still able to accommodate the wishes of the people who elected them, whereas their counterparts in Gmünd are obliged to leave much of what used to be their responsibility to the mercy of market forces.

VI. According to neoliberal doctrine, the market is the most effective instrument for promoting the good of all, and if there is such a thing as the "common good", then it is the good of the largest possible number of individuals. But in Western tradition it is the government, and its instrument the state, that is responsible for the common good. The majority of people are made most vividly aware of this at the local community level. This is why local communities are schools for democracy. Many local residents regard the municipal park as **their** park. If too many trees – or the wrong trees – are cut down, there is a public outcry followed by a public debate, which spills over into the town council. Those who are affected want to have their say, and are free to do so. For many people the department of works is something that belongs to them: they are dependent on its efficient functioning, and its commercial fortunes are not a matter of indifference to them. The public sector, especially at the local community level, belongs to the "realm of citizenship". (ibid., p.357) Privatizations serve to constrict that realm. Citizens have no more say in matters where previously they had a voice.

And even when a privatization is successful, what people gain as customers or consumers they lose as citizens of the state. It may well be that they accept this trade-off. But this does not alter the fact that democracy loses out precisely where it is most easily learned: in the local community. Hence the study is finding that privatization discourages democratic participation.

In industrial nations with a democratic tradition the effects of privatization are felt in a waning of interest in local politics, a lower turn-out in local government elections, and above all in a growing reluctance to stand as a candidate in such elections. We are now seeing more and more examples of experienced local politicians – and possibly more women than men – withdrawing from public life because the few things over which they still have power of decision are not worth the time and mental strain involved.

The fact that the remit of local government is shrinking need not grieve economists. But it will grieve those who see democracy as a self-contained value in its own right, at least as important as prosperity. For developing countries, where the state first of all has to be "built" (Fukuyama), rigorous privatization means that in the very place where democratic "nation-building" needs to begin, there is very little opportunity for this to happen.

Shared responsibility for the water supply can encourage a village or small town in Africa to do remarkable things, which can then become the starting point for a democratic engagement. If decisions about the water supply are made by someone far away in France or America, this only goes to prove once again how little the ordinary people in the "dark continent" count, and the extent to which they are the object of decisions rather than the subject.

The constitutional state does not exist in a vacuum. It represents one dimension of the state, a state that must be constructed, fashioned and supported by its citizens. And for them to do this they need to know and see for themselves that this is their state, that it is about them, their quality of life and their future. So now, in the wake of the twin tides of nationalization and privatization, we need a proper European debate about what the market can and should do, and whether it really **should** do all the things that, at a pinch, it perhaps can do. And about what can sensibly be called the function of the state: that it is more than just the frying pan in which the economists can fry their fish, while wondering how and where they can pick up a cheaper frying pan.

VII. This debate will need to begin at the point where privatization touches the core area of the state's responsibility: its monopoly on the use of force. Is it all right to privatize prisons? Prisons are there to accommodate people who have forfeited their basic right to freedom of movement for a specific period of time, and in some cases for life. In a constitutional state only an independent judge, acting on the basis of a law, can deprive a person of his freedom. Punishing crimes, judging people and passing sentence on them, is the sole right of the state. It is the state that builds prisons, trains and appoints officials to carry out the sentence imposed by a court "in the name of the people".

Everyone will surely agree that the making of laws and the dispensation of justice cannot be privatized. So is it possible to privatize the execution of a judicial verdict? Can private companies lock people up on behalf of the state?

The answer from the United States is an unequivocal "yes". It started back in 1982, when the governor of the state of New York, Mario Cuomo, went to the urban development corporation with the request to build not just housing for the poor, as they had been doing, but also prisons. Harsh anti-drugs laws had landed many people in prison who had previously got away with a fine. The prisons were full to bursting, and not just in New York State. This is one of the reasons why the US prison population increased fourfold in the 25 years from 1980 to 2005. In 1980 the prison population numbered around half a million, by 2005 it was 2.1 million. How can the state accommodate and guard two million prisoners? Answer: by privatizing the prison system. A whole new fast-growing industry has come into being, which undertakes to organize the locking-up of criminals for anything between 4 per cent and 14 per cent less money than the state, and to build prison accommodation more quickly. Starting in 1991, private companies have created cells for 100,000 prisoners in the state of Texas in just a matter of years.

This is not the place to catalogue all the disadvantages and abuses that have resulted from this privatization. After all, things are not that great in state-run prisons either. However, two of the negative consequences clearly have nothing to do with human failings, but with the actual system of privatized prisons as such.

In Europe jurists and politicians are divided on the issue of how far a prison sentence should be seen as atonement for crimes committed, and how far as an opportunity for reformation – or in other words, what role rehabilitation and reintegration into society should play. But they are all agreed that reintegration is an important aim.

Private prisons have no interest in this. Firstly because it adds to costs and lowers shareholder value. And secondly because it is in the interest of private prisons to be run at full capacity, so they are quite happy to have prisoners coming back inside soon after their release.

Between 1993 and 2000, the years of rapid privatization, the average prison stay in US prisons increased from 12 to 17 months. There are observers who see a connection between this and the interest of private companies to keep prisoners for as long as possible. Who is going to decide, in a private prison, whether someone should be released early for good behavior?

Of course, one must be careful not to make simplistic connections between cause and effect. The prison population as a proportion of the total population is not ten times higher in the US than in the European Union because the "prison-industrial complex" that we now hear so much about has an interest in keeping it that way. Nor does one have to believe those who claim the entire justice system is already under the influence of this "complex". But if the power of this new industry should turn out to be in any way responsible, however minimally, for that alarming figure of two million prisoners, then there are clearly very practical as well as ethical arguments to be made against privatized prisons. And the practical arguments are bound up with the ethical ones. It cannot be right for the state to delegate parts of its monopoly on the use of force, and indeed the enforcement of its laws, to private companies that will only be around as long as there are profits to be made. It is in the interests of a constitutional state that as few of its citizens as possible commit a criminal offence. But for someone who has invested money in private prisons, the fear is that one day there will be too few of them. The idea that a human being, even a single solitary human being, might be sitting in jail because other people are making money out of it, is simply intolerable. It makes a mockery of the constitutional state. And the constitutional state, even according to Milton Friedman, is more important than privatization.

VIII. Operating even closer to the nerve of the state, its monopoly on the use of force, are all those who seek to privatize internal security. Preventing, fighting and punishing crime is the duty and right of the state. If what happens **after** the judge passes sentence is not amenable to privatization, what about everything that precedes sentencing?

In the US and elsewhere, private security firms are a growth industry. In Germany there were 620 such companies offering their services in 1984. By 1996 there were 1800, and by 2003 the number had risen to 2500, employing around 160,000 people. Many are performing traditional tasks such as guarding factory premises; but the number of private individuals and families who are now paying for their personal security is growing rapidly. Admittedly the legal status of private security personnel in Germany is not comparable with that of the police. They may only use force if they are attacked (self-defense) or if they are trying to prevent a law-breaker – a shoplifter, say – from fleeing.

In June 1999 the city of Frankfurt entered into an agreement with nine out of a total of 80 security firms based in the city, entrusting them with responsibility for policing security on the underground rail network. Another firm was given the right to guard car parks and collect parking charges. The Frankfurt police accorded their new helpers the status of an auxiliary police force, with the right to monitor illegal parking.

By September 1999, after just three months, the Frankfurt city council decided to end the experiment with effect from 1 January 2002. It had been nothing but trouble. The first bone of contention was the uniform. Most Frankfurt residents wanted the uniforms worn by the auxiliaries to be clearly distinguishable from those of the regular police force. Then it turned out that the private security personnel, unaccustomed to dealing with members of the public, reacted more violently, when in doubt, than the better trained police. They were also unfamiliar with the electronic registration system. But the main problem was that the expected cost savings failed to materialize. The whole scheme cost 10 per cent more than if the police had handled everything themselves. So things went back to the way they were before: private security firms now protect shops in the city centre or private clients out in the suburbs.

Afterwards local residents were asked which of 16 different functions they thought could safely be delegated to private operators. The answer was "none". The survey also revealed a fundamental rejection of the concept, with 69.4 per cent of respondents taking the view that the privatization of security is socially unjust. They felt it would lead to a two-tier security society. They agreed with the statement "Private security serves and protects only the rich". (Ernst Ulrich von Weizsäcker, Oran R. Young and Matthias Finger, *Limits to Privatization. How to Avoid too Much of a Good Thing*, London 2005, p.168) The people whose job it is to protect the wealthy first and foremost are themselves abjectly poor for the most part. In Great Britain they earn about half the wage of an industrial worker. A more fertile breeding-ground for corruption it would be hard to imagine.

IX. The privatization of internal security finds its logical conclusion in the gated communities of the USA, Brazil and South Africa. This is not the place to revisit an earlier account of the self-exclusion of the wealthy. For this see my book *Vom Gewaltmonopol zum Gewaltmarkt* (Frankfurt/Main 2002).

In the US, perhaps, the proliferation of cities within cities, ringed by walls like the imperial cities of the Middle Ages, secured by electric fences and protected by privately hired guards, has something to do with what de Tocqueville so admired about the Americans: their ability to band together, independently of the state authorities, to build a school, establish a playground, combat alcohol consumption, in short: to take the welfare of the community into their own hands. Except that in the case of these fortified enclaves, to which nobody is admitted without a special pass or a special invitation, it is no longer about the welfare of the community at large, but only about the welfare of those who have paid good money to buy their place inside the "gated community". The difference between being inside and outside is far greater than if one were to cross the border today between Germany and France, or between Germany and the Czech Republic. And particularly where gated communities are established to protect residents against the inhabitants of nearby slums we find two separate worlds, which have very little to do with each other – apart from the fact that the state monopoly on the use of force no longer applies in either. The slums are run by criminal gangs, the gated communities by private security firms. The former challenge the authority of the state, the latter take its place.

So it is only logical that people living in these urban fortresses – in South Africa they call them "citadels" – should now start to call for exemption from local taxes. What the local authority would otherwise have to do, the residents now organize for themselves. In a sense they are a community apart, and much more sharply divided from their neighbors than communities normally are. Why should they pay taxes to the outside world?

Margaret Thatcher's dictum, that there is no such thing as society, has here been put into practice. Instead of society there are social enclaves, where people join together and organize to represent and defend their special interests. And this they should be allowed to do (according to the Thatcherites), without regard for some imaginary, larger society, and especially without regard for the state, which is there to represent, order, protect and nurture this larger society.

Wherever states disintegrate – and we shall see this in Chapter 7 – the privatization of violence goes hand in hand with the decline and fall of the state. The one drives the other. Is the privatization of internal security in industrial nations a harbinger of their decline and fall too? Can a state delegate its monopoly on the use of force? Where security becomes a commodity, is there anything left that we can call a "state", as we have understood the term since 1648? Can security be put on a shopping list of values, like a Mercedes car, which some people can afford and others not? Is it not the job of the state to prevent exactly this from happening?

X. Sociologist Trutz von Trotha sees the worldwide advent of a "preventive security order", following the collapse of the state monopoly on the use of force. And because he sees this as a fact of life that we must get used to, he uses the abbreviation PSO: "The PSO is an order of manifest social and cultural inequality, segregation and differences that spell conflict. It shares these features with the order of commoditized violence. The PSO replaces the duty of the state to take responsibility for the life and property of its citizens with the purchasing power of the buyer in the market for 'security assets'." (Trutz von Trotha, "Die präventive Sicherheitsordnung, in: Werner Ruf, *Politische Ökonomie der Gewalt: Staatszerfall und die Privatisierung von Gewalt und Krieg*, Opladen 2003, p.63)

What von Trotha calls "the order of commoditized violence" is what remains when states disintegrate, or in other words what the French no longer regard as order at all, but as an *entité chaotique*.

That von Trotha has something similar in mind can be seen from the continuation of his argument: "The prerogative of power is replaced by the primacy of the market. And part of that is that the PSO translates the pattern of economic inequality into the social inequality of security provision. If the state order operates on the principle of 'equal security for all', the PSO follows the precept 'equal security for all who can afford it'. Its motto is: 'Pay up or get robbed!'" (ibid., p.63)

Anyone who can present other people with the choice "Pay up or get robbed!" obviously wields power. But – unlike the modern constitutional state – not a power that is subject to the law.

Von Trotha reminds us of Hans Magnus Enzensberger's essay *Aussichten auf den Bürgerkrieg* (Frankfurt/Main 1993), which, following the end of the Cold War, foresaw the advent of a global civil war that would "literally be about nothing". (Hans Magnus Enzensberger, *Aussichten auf den Bürgerkrieg* (Frankfurt/Main 1993, p.35) Even back then Enzensberger had already noted: "On the one hand we get protected zones with their own security services, on the other slums and ghettoes. In the abandoned parts of town official agencies, police patrols and the courts no longer have any say. These areas are out of control." (ibid., p.55)

For von Trotha, the privatization of violence from the top down and from the bottom up does not yet herald the arrival of a primitive Hobbesian state of chaotic violence, where all are at war with each other. But he too sounds a warning note: "The irresponsible ideological flirtation with fantasies of a market-based society and with the privatization of the core of modern statehood, especially the monopoly on the use of force, is quite literally 'playing with fire'. The burning cars, the looted stores and the fury of young people in the run-down suburban estates of North America and Western Europe – these are its signs." (Trutz von Trotha, "Die präventive Sicherheitsordnung, in: Werner Ruf, *Politische Ökonomie der Gewalt: Staatszerfall und die Privatisierung von Gewalt und Krieg*, Opladen 2003, p.72)

XI. The idea that war could be privatized was still unthinkable at the time of the Cold War. With the end of that war, army establishments were cut. Hundreds of thousands of soldiers in the East and West lost their jobs. Among them were many who had learned no other trade apart from war, and had no desire to learn anything else.

And so, after an interval of 200 years, we witnessed the resurgence of mercenary warfare. The conscripted armies of the nation-states shrank in size until conscription existed only on paper – and was abolished altogether in many states. Wars between European states were no longer a possibility, and if the military was needed at all, it was generally only on the margins or outside Europe, and then for tasks that really should have been handled by the police, except that the police evidently could not cope.

The fact that democratic states now find it hard to send their soldiers – even though they are volunteers – to regions ruled by the chaos of commodified violence is one of the reasons why the 1990s saw the birth of "private military companies" (PMCs). A few of these are quite large, most of them are small. The first and for a long time the largest of these organizations was recruited from former South African soldiers and policemen, and led by a retired South African staff officer. It called itself "Executive Outcomes" (EO), a name that meant little to the uninitiated, but a great deal to those in the business. EO hired out mercenary units to states or companies who were able to pay for their services. In the absence of hard currency, EO took payment in the form of mining rights or other rights to the exploitation of natural resources. Its principal area of operations was black Africa. EO mercenaries were regarded as more reliable, more disciplined and above all more effective as a fighting force than the regular African military. Established in 1989, Executive Outcomes was wound up only ten years later, but it lived on in another PMC, called "Sandline International", which sounds even less military than "Executive Outcomes".

While EO, Sandline International and many smaller companies operate freely in the marketplace, deciding for themselves who they will work for, another large enterprise called "Military Professional Resources Inc." (MPRI) is closely associated with the US Department of Defense. Led by former US officers, it is mainly staffed by discharged US Army soldiers. What we have here is a form of outsourcing, of the kind that has become standard in industry. MPRI is free to work for other clients, but doubtless only if the Pentagon agrees, and sometimes because the Pentagon wants it to. But for the most part MPRI carries out tasks that the Pentagon would rather entrust to it than to the US Army.

Soon after entering office, American Defense Secretary Donald Rumsfeld gave a clear signal by insisting that everything that was not part of the military's core function must be outsourced. For the Defense Secretary this has more than one advantage. For one thing, private contractors are not subject to military jurisdiction and are therefore not bound by the rules of war. So they can be used for missions of a more delicate nature. Secondly, any casualties suffered by such contractors are treated more as workplace accidents, and need not be viewed as an occasion for national mourning. The Secretary's dread of the first zinc coffin, draped in the national flag, is lessened. It is also in the interests of the US that nobody to this day can say with certainty whether or not American assistance, rendered through MPRI, was instrumental in the swift reconquest of Kraina by the Croats.

From the MPRI website we learn that the company employs 800 people, while the "workforce" can draw on a pool of 12,000 "professionals" recruited from the army and the police. Under the heading "Mission" we find the unexceptionable claim: "We serve the needs of the US government, of international law enforcement organizations and of the private sector with highest standards and cost-effective solutions."

Similar claims could be made by another large company close to the Pentagon, the military corporation "Dyn Corp", which is based in Reston, Virginia, a satellite town of Washington DC. Dyn Corp has adopted as its motto: "Dynamic, dedicated, driven".

Naturally MPRI, Dyn Corp and many others participated in the Iraq war, contributing a substantial "workforce". The figures, all of them unofficial, vary. But it seems certain that the "coalition of the billing" – meaning these and other private companies hired and paid by the Pentagon – is larger than the "coalition of the willing", which consists mainly of British troops, but also included Polish, Italian, Australian, and initially Spanish contingents as well. One company alone, Erinys International, maintains a private army in Iraq consisting of 1500 South Africans and 14,000 Iraqi guards. Like a number of NATO states, the company trains Iraqi security personnel. "Blackwater USA", another security company with 450 personnel in Iraq, announces on its website: "We have the people to carry out any mission." This is entirely credible, since one in four of its employees is an ex-member of the Chilean army discharged for involvement in human rights abuses.

The four Americans who were lynched in Faluja on 31 March 2004 also worked for Blackwater. In the media they were classed as "civilians". In fact the "civilian" mercenaries were more hated by the Iraqis than the regular soldiers. They were also involved in the torture of Iraqi prisoners. But we hear nothing about any legal proceedings against them. Which court would have jurisdiction over them?

XII. So what **are** the objections to delegating military tasks to a company that – quite plausibly – offers "cost-effective solutions"? If, as they say, "what is good for General Motors is good for America", then should the state be allowed to do what General Motors regards it as right and profitable to do? And in particular, should the state be allowed to do it in an area where it must have, and retain, a monopoly, namely in the use of force? Is it right that in a war, such as the one in Iraq, the state should hand out 48.7 billion dollars to 150 private firms – approximately the sum that Germany spends each year on its armed forces?

The constitutional state is supposed to be the instrument whereby every use of force – private, privatized and state-authorized – is subjected to the rule of law. So is it entirely proper for the state itself to create legal grey areas? It is true that secret services also operate within such grey areas. But that is precisely why, in constitutional states, they are not permitted to use force themselves. A republic is a *res publica*, a public matter. Hence the fact that the state's monopoly on the use of force, both at home and abroad, can only be legitimized if it is subject to public control. It cannot be hived off and delegated to private enterprise.

There is no need to doubt the will or the ability of the Pentagon to keep private contractors under strict control. And this is what distinguishes this partial privatization of war from the state

99

sponsorship of militias and paramilitaries that we see in places like Colombia, Serbia, Indonesia or the Sudan. It is true that in America too the semi-private mercenary armies were formed not without the help of the government, true also that successive administrations were keen to distance themselves from direct responsibility for dubious ventures. And both are examples of the same process, namely the "privatization of violence from the top down", albeit with the important difference that the paramilitary groups, once they have access to their own sources of funding and have built up an economy based on violence, could not care less about the government to which they owe their existence. And as a result they very quickly adapt their fighting methods to those of the forces they were set up to combat. At this point they have no more interest in a state that could only disrupt their business operations and punish their atrocities. Even less desirable for them is any form of peace, which could deprive them of their livelihood.

As far as anyone can judge, the companies with which the Pentagon works cannot go down this road. They remain bound by the instructions of their government paymasters. So this is about a partial privatization of war, as opposed to the privatization and commercialization of violence *per se* in the case of the paramilitaries. In the first case the line that defines the state monopoly on the use of force becomes blurred, while in the second this monopoly is itself negated and destroyed. But what Peter Lock has formulated as a "general rule" is equally applicable to both: "That the privatization of security is a mirror of the condition of statehood and social cohesion." (Peter Lock, "War Economies and the Shadow of Globalisation", in: Werner Ruf, *Politische Ökonomie der Gewalt: Staatszerfall und die Privatisierung von Gewalt und Krieg*, Opladen 2003, p.117)

Chapter 6
War and the State

I. By 1648 the right to wage war (*jus ad bellum*), together with the monopoly on the use of force, had come to define and constitute the sovereign state. Internally the state had the right to enforce its laws, with violence if necessary; and externally it had the right to wage war. For a long time that right was unfettered, and it extended to wars of aggression.

The liberal use made of that right over centuries by the European states is astonishing to a younger generation for whom a European war is no longer conceivable. Dynastic wars of succession, wars of hegemony, wars of liberation, wars of unification, wars of conquest – these have shaped European history for three hundred years, from 1648 to 1945. And it all ended in a barbaric war of annihilation that lasted from 1941 to 1945.

These wars inflicted unspeakable suffering upon the peoples of Europe, despite the fact that as late as the 18th century respectable citizens wanted nothing to do with the business of war. But these same wars have made the state more powerful. In time of war the peasant in Normandy or in the Palatinate sensed that the count who lived in the castle above the neighboring village was not the highest authority in the land. That was the king or the electoral prince, and when he was at war, so were all his subjects with him. Then foreign soldiers might come looting and plundering, burning down homes and farms. So people needed soldiers of their own, a state that could defend itself. The myth of Prussia, which was still being co-opted by the Nazis, was born during the Seven Years War. What made the French so attached to their own state at the beginning of the 20th century was not least the desire to expunge the humiliation of 1871.

In no previous war had the state encroached so far on the lives of its citizens as in the First World War. The state determined what women and children "on the home front" got to eat, what the factories were to produce, who was conscripted to the military and when, who was classed as "indispensable to the war effort" and allowed to stay at home. Government agencies decided which newspaper reports gave succor to the enemy, which editorials weakened morale, which book titles would be allocated paper for printing, and which would not.

When a nation is fighting for its very existence, everyone is judged according to what he contributes to the struggle. The state has, and uses, the means to urge and compel each individual to make the contribution that some authority or other deems him capable of making. With the idea of total war, Colonel General Erich Ludendorff also prefigured the total state.

The dictators of the 1920s and 30s then proceeded to build on this, even in peacetime. Anyone listening to the rhetoric of the National Socialists in the 21st century might well conclude that this was a continuation of war by other means. From morning till night the cheap "People's Receiver" radios, which could only receive broadcasts from the local state radio station, blared out talk of "struggle", "sacrifice" and "discipline", while the "will to fight", "readiness for action" and "certainty of victory" were celebrated, and employers and employees became "works leaders and their loyal followers". The adjective "fanatical" carried no negative overtones, and "fanaticism" was a virtue. But then it was all or nothing, victory or defeat. To a later observer the outbreak of the Second World War appears as a predictable consequence, almost a return to normal. Hitler had accused imperial Germany of losing the war only because it had been too lily-livered, had failed to mobilize all available resources, and had not put a sufficient number of "defeatists and back-stabbers" up against the wall. Now he planned to do better.

One thing is clear: the fact that the power of the state got out of hand, that in the end people existed for the state and not the other way round, had to do with the wars, and especially the First World War. But this also implies that a state in time of peace is necessarily going to look different from a state that has either emerged from a war, or is preparing to fight one. Its responsibilities, its style, its methods will be different. Above all: the dangers it faces are likely to come from a different quarter.

II. In the 1950s, when the threat of an atomic war was very real, the physicist and philosopher Carl Friedrich von Weizsäcker stated baldly that if humanity wanted to have a future, it must "outgrow the institution of war". The capacity for mutually assured destruction made the concept of a *jus ad bellum* appear absurd. By the "institution of war" Weizsäcker clearly meant the phenomenon that had afflicted Europe repeatedly for 300 years, namely wars between states. Only states had access to atomic weapons of mass destruction. And even a war that began with conventional weapons could escalate to an atomic Armageddon. Weizsäcker did not exclude the possibility that people would carry on shooting at each other, killing each other, contrary to the laws of their land.

The unification of Europe shows how realistic the physicist's call to abolish war was. The very continent that has been most plagued by wars is well on the way to abolishing war between states as an institution. The last wars to be fought in Europe are currently the subject of war crimes tribunals in The Hague. Perhaps it will take future generations to appreciate the full extent of Europe's achievement in making war history.

Wars in other parts of the world are still possible, but they are becoming increasingly unlikely. India and Pakistan are learning that they are condemned to peace by their own atomic weapons. North Korea knows that an attack on South Korea could well unleash the American military machine, and South Korea has time on its side. The dictatorship of the Kim dynasty in the North will not last forever.

But what about Iraq? Is not the "pre-emptive strike" part of US military doctrine? And if the US, as the hegemonic power of our day, follows this doctrine, must not war – meaning war between states – become normal again, an instrument of politics like any other?

The Iraq war would have been only the first in a series of hegemonic wars, had it produced the outcome that former Vice President Dick Cheney or former Deputy Defense Secretary Paul Wolfowitz dreamed of: a peaceful, democratic, US-friendly Iraq, where US oil firms can pursue their oil business in peace. But however the future of Iraq turns out, it will not be like that.

Generally speaking, war between states today does not even benefit the victor. The story does not end with the use of force by the victor nation: it continues with the denationalized, privatized violence unleashed inside the defeated country. Military victory leads to the erosion of the state monopoly on the use of force, especially if the victor is stupid enough, as in Iraq, to abolish the state. It takes the US a few weeks to destroy a state by military force. Constructing a new one takes decades. Those few weeks are inordinately costly. The ensuing decades are costlier still.

The fact that every avoidable war is a crime is unlikely to worry hard-boiled ideologues. What does give them pause is the fact that it is a loss-making business, both politically and economically.

The idea of war between states has not been vindicated in Iraq, but reduced to absurdity. Far from triumphing, unilateralism has failed. An international monopoly on the use of force could relieve pressure even on the US hegemony, as soon as it realizes that it could do with this relief. And that realization is growing.

III. All the talk about war, all the fear of war, all the struggle against war in the 20th century was founded on a premise that nobody thought about because it seemed self-evident: that there is a clear-cut distinction between war and peace. Not only could one tell the difference between war and peace without having to think about it, they were absolute opposites. Prior to 1 August 1914, peace reigned in Europe – peace, prosperity and freedom of movement. When the German Empire declared war on Russia and France, Europe was at war, and with war came fear, grief and hunger. Ambassadors handed over their notes and departed. Armies were mobilized. It was no longer a crime to kill other people, but an act of heroism for the fatherland.

But even for the clearly defined legal situation of war there were rules. It was clear who was authorized to shoot and who was not. The death penalty awaited those who were not authorized to shoot – because they were not soldiers in uniform – but who nevertheless did so. There were rules about how to surrender, and about how prisoners were to be treated. Sometimes the rules were broken, but they remained in force, unchallenged, until 1941, when Hitler suspended them in advance of the attack on the Soviet Union.

In the 21st century we are growing accustomed to the proliferation of conflicts and outbreaks of violence that certainly do not correspond to our traditional notions of "peace", but which equally fail to meet the definition of "war" as used in international law or the law of war. Is there a war going on in Palestine? In a country where there is only one army, namely the Israeli army, while the Palestinians do not even have a state yet? Was the bloodbath in Rwanda a war? Or just a massacre? Is there a war going on at present on the border between Rwanda and the Congo? And what about Sudan? Is what the Arab militia are doing to the black Sudanese "war"? Is it civil war? Or is it something else again: privatized violence?

Of course, one can evade the question just by labeling all acts of violence as "New Wars". But where then is the dividing line between war and organized criminality? Is it a crime if five gangsters attack a hotel, but a war when fifty gangsters terrorize a small town?

Certainly there are new kinds of wars, and there is no reason why they should not be dubbed "New Wars". What went on in Kosovo were acts of war carried out by NATO against a state, albeit one that was terrorizing and driving out its own citizens by military means, and that delegated a part of its monopoly on the use of force to criminals such as "Arkan's Tigers". As NATO wanted at all costs to avoid casualties on its own side – in which it succeeded – it confined itself to high-altitude air attacks beyond the reach of the Serbian air defenses. So it was a highly asymmetric war, but a war of states (plural) against a single state. What former President Bush ordered in Iraq was also a highly asymmetric war, in which those who were attacked stood not the slightest chance: but it was a war between states.

And is what then began in Iraq still "war"? When suicide bombers mingle with a crowd of young people waiting to apply for a job in the police, in order to blow up themselves and a dozen "traitors" – is that war? Or civil war?

In the last 350 years the Europeans have got used to the idea that war has something to do with the state. War is either armed conflict between states, or else – in the form of civil war – it is the armed struggle for power within a state. Such was the case in Spain between 1936 and 1939. The same could be said of the Ivory Coast today, where rival factions are fighting for power in Abidjan. Even though the rebels in the north of the country wanted to set up their own state, the term "civil war" still seems appropriate. But when nobody knows any more who is fighting whom, and who is killing people for what reason – and that was the case in the Congo, where more than two million people died, mostly women and children – it makes sense to talk not about "war", but about violence, privatized, denationalized, and for the most part commercialized violence. One form of this violence is what ministers of the interior define and combat as "terror", although it should be pointed out that the terror perpetrated by warlords or bands of murderous thugs, paramilitaries and death squads has claimed, and continues to claim, thousands of times more victims than what Bush tried to target with his "war on terror".

IV. This privatized and commercialized violence operates according to entirely different rules from those that apply to war proper. Wars are always immensely costly for states. Privatized violence also has to pay its way. Political scientist Herfried Münkler has described in detail how the economics of this kind of violence work. Someone who makes a business out of violence, earning his living – and more – from violence, has no interest in peace. So privatized violence, unlike wars, has no definable beginning or end, but tends rather towards a condition of permanence. Regular soldiers want to return home again as soon as possible: mercenaries hired by warlords fear unemployment.

Wars have clearly defined front lines. Privatized violence thrives on the fact that it can never be pinned down, and can strike anywhere. Wars have rules, privatized violence throws out the rulebook. In wars dictators have been known to send fifteen-year-olds to the front as a desperate last resort. Warlords, on the other hand, use thirteen-year-olds as a first resort, since the death of a child costs them less money than the death of an experienced mercenary.

The law of war seeks to confine the conflict to the armed forces of the states involved – to spare civilians, in other words. Privatized violence is directed primarily at civilians, especially women and children. Battles between mercenaries are avoided as far as possible, because they only add to the costs. Soldiers learn to distinguish between combatants and non-combatants.

Privatized violence distinguishes only between people who still have something worth taking – and those who have nothing more to give.

Of course, it is possible to stretch the definition of any concept. And it is true that there were wars before the birth of the modern state. It can also be argued – with a sideways glance at Clausewitz – that the nature and form of warfare have changed in the course of history.

This metamorphosis is invoked by Herfried Münkler, who makes the most persuasive and consistent case for extending the definition of "war": "A definition of war that seeks to capture its very essence, and not just a particular manifestation in time and space, must be sufficiently flexible to embrace the changing forms of war and the multiplicity of forms that war has taken. This is normally done by adding a qualifying epithet or phrase, as in "partisan war", "people's war", "cabinet war", "war of succession", "war of conquest", "war of devastation", "colonial war", "war of pacification". (Herfried Münkler, "Krieg", in: Gerhard Göhler, Mattias Iser, Ina Kerner (eds.), *Politische Theorie. 22 umkämpfte Begriffe zur Einführung*, Wiesbaden 2005, p.228)

What Münkler overlooks is the fact that all these forms of war have something in common: all of them, directly or indirectly, are wars between states. It is states that colonize, states that pacify. Even the partisan wars of the Second World War in Russia, the Ukraine, Serbia were parts of a war between states. The Russian partisans thought of themselves as part of the armed forces who were called upon to throw the German invaders out of the country. They fought behind the front as others fought at the front – and for a state, the Russian state, even if not all of them risked their lives for the Soviet state.

V. The outbreaks of violence reported in the media today are not wars between states, nor in many cases are they civil wars fought to gain power within a state. This violence is not only de-nationalized and not authorized by the state: in most cases it is also fundamentally anti-state. Those who combine business with violence, who promote their business by means of violence and use that business to finance further violence, do not want the state at all, and cannot possibly want it. So there is something else going on here that makes it different from all the forms of war listed by Münkler.

In the end Münkler comes to this remarkable conclusion: "In order to encompass the extraordinarily diverse forms of war, we must abandon the attempt to define the meaning of 'war' in the singular." (ibid., p.228) So Münkler does not have a broader definition of his own to set against the traditional definition, which sees war as an armed conflict between states or (in the form of civil war) the armed struggle for power within a state. He gives up on the attempt to define war. But if one cannot, with the best will in the world, say what is a war and what is not, is there any point in talking about "New Wars"? This presupposes, after all, that there is something here which, for all its mutability, does have a definable core.

Clausewitz compared war to a chameleon, but of course a chameleon is not an indefinable something, but a very specific creature, which has the ability to assume different shapes. Something that cannot be defined cannot be differentiated from other things. So is it really not possible to differentiate war from organized crime and gangland criminality?

It is hardly surprising that there is now an academic debate going on about the concept of "New Wars" – a fairly sterile argument about what is actually so new about these "wars", and whether we have not seen similar things in the past. Ulrich Teusch, for example, gave a radio talk on the subject on 20 February 2005 (Südwest Rundfunk II). Much more important are the doubts about whether the definition of war can be stretched as far as Münkler stretches it without the meanings of words becoming totally confused. This is the question addressed in the book *Kriege als (Über)Lebenswelten. Schattenglobalisierung, Kriegsökonomien und Inseln der Zivilität* edited by Sabine

Kurtenbach and Peter Lock. In the foreword by Lothar Brock we read: "The thesis of the editors is that under these conditions the dichotomy 'war versus non-war' can no longer be sustained. They therefore propose that the concept of war be dropped." (Lothar Brock, "Vorwort", in: Sabine Kurtenbach, Peter Lock (eds.), *Kriege als (Über)Lebenswelten. Schattenglobalisierung, Kriegsökonomien und Inseln der Zivilität*, Bonn 2004, p.17) We need (he continues) "to get past the narrow focus on 'war' when analyzing the concept of armed force. This view is supported by the fact that the day-to-day lives of entire population groups can be affected far more by criminal violence than by the use of military force." (ibid., p.16)

Brock cites the introductory essay by Sabine Kurtenbach and Peter Lock in support of his argument. Their conclusion: "It is becoming increasingly difficult to differentiate between war and a prevailing climate of violent criminality. Given the high rates of territorially concentrated criminal violence in highly fragmented societies such as Nigeria, South Africa or Brazil, it is not even possible to use victim numbers as a differentiating marker."

The authors are referring to the number of victims in places like Sao Paulo or Rio de Janeiro. The gang wars in these cities, which are usually about control of the drugs trade, are analyzed by British anthropologist Luke Dowdney: "The rivalries there claim thousands of victims each year, including many children who kill and get killed, like the child soldiers of warlords." (Sabine Kurtenbach, Peter Lock (eds.), *Kriege als (Über)Lebenswelten. Schattenglobalisierung, Kriegsökonomien und Inseln der Zivilität*, Bonn 2004, p.213 ff.)

At least the academic community, too, is now starting to ask itself where it makes sense to speak of "war", and where it is more appropriate to speak simply of "violence": "To broaden the focus of analysis once more by shifting our attention away from war and onto violence." (Lothar Brock, "Vorwort", in: Sabine Kurtenbach, Peter Lock (eds.), *Kriege als (Über)Lebenswelten. Schattenglobalisierung, Kriegsökonomien und Inseln der Zivilität*, Bonn 2004, p.15)

VI. Academics are fairly free when it comes to differentiating between the meanings of terms. But what might be just a theoretical argument about words for a historian, sociologist or political scientist, in which one can find good reasons for taking this line or that, prompts a politician to ask what effects such a definition – or non-definition – might have and what actions can, and perhaps must, result from it.

The terms we use shape our thoughts, they determine what we are able to take in and understand, but also what we – perhaps inevitably – misunderstand. Depending on the words and concepts with which we approach what we call "reality", that reality changes. What we experience and perceive as reality determines our actions. So our language, the terms we use, anticipate our actions.

The politician needs to make distinctions in order to act. And he needs to make the right distinctions in order to act in the right way. The terms "war" and "state" have hitherto been intimately linked. Whoever severs that link must reflect first – not as a scientist or academic, but as a politically responsible citizen – on the consequences, not the consequences for historiography, but for the future of his own society.

If the terms "war" and "state" are connected in the minds of people – and have been for 350 years – then a redefinition of war also affects the state, or to be more precise, our conception of the state. If war becomes undefinable, does this mean that the state can no longer be defined either? What kind of a state is it in which anyone who tries to make his living with a Kalashnikov can claim that he is waging war? The objection that it depends on the number of Kalashnikovs and their victims will not wash. Is there peace in Sao Paulo as long as fewer than five thousand people are killed in a year – but war if the number goes above five thousand, which it sometimes does?

Whoever rules a state must defend its monopoly on the use of force. Those who infringe that monopoly must be prosecuted as law-breakers, those who brazenly flout it must be indicted as criminals. Anyone who privatizes the use of force that properly belongs to the state, and does so against the will of the state, turning it into a commodity to be bought and sold, is a criminal in the eyes of the state, and not a warrior. It makes no difference whether we are talking about organized crime, terror born of ideological conviction, or the secession of a warlord. The rulers of a state must distinguish between legitimate and illegitimate violence. Every state must stand or fall by this distinction. It is integral to the very definition of the state.

It follows that those who write about the privatization and commercialization of violence in (for example) black Africa in terms of "New Wars" have already written off the modern state with its monopoly on the use of force. Such writers like to point out that wars very different from those fought after 1648 also occurred in the Middle Ages. Indeed they did – for the simple reason that the modern state did not yet exist. And such wars can only occur today when and where this state no longer exists, or at any rate when it is on the point of disintegration.

VII. Everything has its day, including the modern state. It is the job of historians to document the rise and fall of an institution. They may also reflect on its end – including the end of the modern state, and the end of its monopoly on the use of force. And this they are now doing. Wolfgang Reinhard does it at the end of his major study *Die Geschichte der Staatsgewalt* (Munich 2001). He can easily imagine "the end of the modern state in its fully developed form". But he also adds that an alternative to the modern state is not in sight. (Wolfgang Reinhard, *Die Geschichte der Staatsgewalt*, Munich 2001, p.508)

This need not alarm historians. But politicians should be worried. Especially when they contemplate our technological civilization, its complexity, and above all its extreme vulnerability. The robber barons of the 14th century could ambush a couple of merchants and make off with whole wagonloads of salt, spices or wine. That was bad enough for the hapless victims. But down the road in the next village, nobody took much notice. How many well-trained terrorists does it take today to cripple the water supply to the Greater Stuttgart area, Berlin's electricity supply, or rail traffic between Cologne and Paris? Imagine what would happen to Intercity train services if half a dozen tiny groups of saboteurs set themselves up along the route, like the robber barons of yesteryear. Or if the Intercity trains had to pass through the domains of several warlords.

It is now possible for a 15-year-old, armed with a shoulder-fired Stinger missile, to shoot down helicopters – or passenger jets as they land or take off. How is air traffic to be maintained in the absence of an enforceable state ban on the free sale of such weapons?

The secret services of the leading NATO nations have been working for some time to track down potential nuclear terrorists. The first nuclear explosion in a major European or US city could make the spectacular crime of September 11 2001 look like a harmless prelude. Nobody knows what chaos the frightened masses throughout the world will then cause. In short: a world of horse-drawn carts, spears and swords can afford privatized violence. A world of nuclear bombs and biological weapons of mass destruction cannot.

Technological progress has condemned us to a monopoly on the use of force. More precisely, we have condemned ourselves, as a result of technological progress, to a monopoly on the use of force and hence to the state. For the only institution that can administer a monopoly on the use of force responsibly and for the common good, that can legitimize and at the same time limit such a monopoly, is the democratic constitutional state.

VIII. Anyone who claims that the words we use shape our perceptions and thus our actions, and who opposes extending the concept of "war" to the point of indefinability because he fears the worst if we do, is well advised to support his case with examples.

A classic, and at the same time alarming example is George W. Bush's "war on terrorism". When Bush proclaimed the "war on terrorism" on 12 September 2001, some commentators noticed that the French President and the German Chancellor chose not to adopt this form of words, speaking instead of the "fight against terror" (or terrorism). This signaled a political difference that is likely to prove decisive over coming decades.

The "war on terrorism" has consequences that were already starting to emerge in September 2001, although it remains unclear to this day which of these were intended and which were not. One intended consequence, certainly, was that the American nation should unite behind its President, who embodied their unshakable will to win.

But was it intended or unintended that Bush inflated the status of an arch-criminal to that of an enemy combatant and an equally matched opponent? Many today still incline to the view that this was an unintended consequence, since the alternative – the idea that Bush actually intended this – would force us to peer into a vertigo-inducing abyss.

Perhaps it really was the intention that the "war on terrorism" should lower the bar to war between states and thus clear the way for the war in Iraq. Possibly it was the intention that more than half of the US population should not view the war in Iraq – already green-lighted by then – as anything really new, but simply as a new phase in a war that had been raging for some time.

Was the war of aggression against Iraq already intended back then, on 12 September 2001? Was the "war on terrorism" a preliminary to what Heribert Prantl summed up in the observation – made even as the bombs were falling on Baghdad – that the USA had abandoned international law and was now acting on the principle that "might is right"? (*Süddeutsche Zeitung*, No.74/2003, p.13)

Did the string-pullers in the White House know what they were doing when they elevated the pursuit of criminals to the status of a war? Did they intend to do what they afterwards had to do: present a real war as a hunt for criminals, with wanted lists and bounties? Did they know, and did they intend, that the effect would be to suspend the law of war? For this law makes no provision for war as the pursuit of criminals, or for "hostile combatants" with no right to humane treatment.

It was doubtless **not** intended that the war in Iraq should fit seamlessly into the Islamic terrorists' view of the world. They justify their criminal actions in part, after all, with the argument that no army in the world is a match for the US military machine, so that terror is the only effective, indeed the only possible means of resistance left to them. Wherever the superiority of this military machine is demonstrated, the terrorists are reinforced in their beliefs. And the number of suicide bombers continues to rise.

Intended or unintended, the consequences of the decision taken on 12 September 2001 have proved dire. They could lead to something like a globalization of the Middle East conflict: on one side a modern, invincible military force, on the other, privatized resistance worldwide, able if necessary to fall back on the ultimate weapon that is not available to the hegemonic power: the suicide bomber, who may, even more incredibly, be a woman.

IX. Elevating the pursuit of criminals to the status of a war also means that areas of responsibility get shifted about. The police are responsible for the pursuit of law-breakers, with the secret services also being involved in cases of terrorism, and the military is responsible for fighting wars. But in Iraq the US military machine has encouraged and revitalized terrorism, feeding it with a constant stream of desperate, radicalized followers prepared to die for their cause. In its war against terror, the most formidable military power in the world by far is like a helpless soldier plagued by gnats, who blasts away with a submachine gun in his bedroom. He is not trained to fight gnats. Others can do the job better, with far less expenditure of effort.

Those who allocate responsibilities also determine the focus of attention. Presenting the fight against terrorism as a – foreign – war distracts attention from conditions in the home country. America as a whole stands on the side of the good in the struggle against evil. So the privatization of violence in the USA itself – which is a different beast, certainly, from what we see in Afghanistan or the Congo – is not even up for discussion. On the contrary, it is business as usual. The sharper the divide between rich and poor, the more quickly protection against crime becomes a commodity, the more quickly the state's monopoly on the use of force becomes eroded from below and from above – from the slums of the big cities and from the gated communities. Whatever else they have been about, wars have always served to distract attention. The "war on terrorism" makes a debate about the future of one's own state appear not only superfluous, but also unpatriotic.

So it all depends on the conceptual framework within which we perceive reality, understand it, and thus interpret it. Those who broaden and over-extend the definition of "war" to the point where it also covers denationalized, privatized, commercialized, and therefore – according to the laws of every state – criminal violence, are no longer in a position to object to Bush's "war on terrorism", the proclamation of which will one day be seen as a clever piece of party political maneuvering – and a decision with fateful consequences for the United States and the world at large: a wrong decision, that may well come to weigh more heavily on the 21st century than the crime of 11 September 2001.

Chapter 7
State Collapse

I. The idea that a state can simply fall apart and cease to exist is difficult for a European to grasp. European history is rich in examples of coups, revolutions, putsches, in all their manifold forms. But afterwards the state – a state – was still there. A different state, perhaps, but a state of some sort nonetheless. Even in the wake of the most radical revolution, the October Revolution in Russia, a new and stronger state – not to say all too strong – was built on the ruins of the old state apparatus. Multi-nation states like the Habsburg Empire have broken up. Their place was quickly taken by new, smaller states, which mostly failed to be what they aspired to be, namely nation-states. But the old state structures remained intact or were swiftly restored. Even if Nazi Germany had won the war, Hitler's desire simply to wipe states like Poland off the map was probably achievable only on a temporary basis, and only by the use of barbaric methods. Such a desire ran contrary to the tide of history. In the 20th century all European nations wanted their own state. And the

Poles were a nation, more decidedly so than others. Even the outsiders among the Allied victors, who wanted to deny the defeated Germans a state of their own in 1945, quickly abandoned the attempt. The only question was what kind of state they should construct in which occupation zones. In Europe the state has not had a quiet life, but its hold on life has been tenacious.

The UN, too, is the product of an agreement between states: its members are not peoples, still less individuals, its members are states, which like to assert their sovereignty from time to time. The United Nations Charter does not envisage proceedings in which it could be established that a given state no longer exists. Hence the fact that while diplomats too can vote in New York, their paymasters can only rule a city, never a country.

II. Of all those who hold political office in Europe, the politicians responsible for development aid were the first to take notice of, and take seriously, the phenomenon of state collapse. Suddenly they no longer had a reliable opposite number to work with at government level. And it was not worth providing rural development aid if armed bands could just turn up at any time to plunder and burn down the villages they had funded. What was the point in spending a lot of money to develop the infrastructure for industrial enterprises, if nobody was then prepared – or able – to invest in the businesses? People only invest where they can have reasonable confidence in legal safeguards. In the *entité chaotique ingouvernable* there are still markets, for drugs, weapons, diamonds, and for people too, especially women, for human organs, and of course for important foodstuffs. But there is no modern economy any more, even if existing businesses are able to buy protection by hiring mercenaries. So it is not surprising that military experts continue to focus almost exclusively on states and their relationships with each other, while Tobias Debiel, Stephan Klingebiel, Andreas Mehler and Ulrich Schneckener introduce their policy paper of January 2005 with the statement: "The failure and collapse of statehood has become the central issue in peace policy and development policy at the start of the 21st century." (Tobias Debiel, Stephan Klingebiel, Andreas Mehler and Ulrich Schneckener, *Between Ignorance and Intervention. Strategies and Dilemmas of External Actors in Fragile States*, Bonn 2005)

How little this has so far penetrated the consciousness of the Western world can be seen from their reaction to the murder of thousands and the expulsion of hundreds of thousands in Darfur. More pressure must be brought to bear on the government of Sudan, we are told, so that it finally puts a stop to the attacks of the Arab militias "loyal to the government" on the non-Arab farming communities in western Sudan. But what does "loyal to the government" mean in the case of African militias? It is true that these paramilitaries were trained by a Sudanese government. The *Janjaweed*, as they styled themselves, were effectively state-sponsored death squads. But operating between them and the government were warlords, tolerated by the state, but pursuing their own agenda. It is the rule, and not the exception, that such militias emancipate themselves from their sponsors and ignore their appeals. And so it is in Sudan.

This is not the place to unpick all the different forces at work in Sudan. Thomas Schmidinger has already done this in a journal article (Thomas Schmidinger, "Sudan – Der Staat als Warlord", in: *Blätter für deutsche und internationale Politik*, No.2/2005, p.194 ff.). In terms of our present concern – the collapse of the state – the only part that matters is the conclusion to which Schmidinger comes: "It is not just in the western part of the country that guerrillas and state-sponsored warlords are fighting each other. In the east, too, armed opposition groups are active. In the autumn of 2004 a new guerrilla group was formed in Kordofan from militias previously loyal to the government. This example shows how quickly even state-supported warlords can turn against their 'creators'. But in the case of Darfur the government itself and its allies are behaving no differently from warlords. An authoritarian government suffering from a serious legitimacy problem only serves to undermine the state. Which is what is happening in Sudan. If the government itself acts increasingly like a warlord, dismantling other state functions – such as social welfare – and retreating into its repressive role as an authoritarian state, it is hardly surprising that the effect is to undermine the very concept of 'statehood'. This weakening of the state, brought about by the state itself, does not just put one particular region at risk: it signals the beginning of the 'Somalization' of the entire state." (ibid., p.200)

It makes a difference whether one views an African conflict through European eyes, and wonders why the government does not impose order, or whether one views it as a stage on the road towards the collapse of the state. If it is true that the Sudanese government is not in essence behaving any differently from the warlords it has supported, and who are now turning against it; if the government now sees itself, more from necessity than choice, as just another player in the poker game of power; then there is little hope for Sudan. For it is part of the mechanism of state collapse that authoritarian regimes, lacking all legitimacy, are no longer perceived by people as the representatives of the public interest, but as just one of several cliques brawling over power and perks.

III. The fact that the states most liable to collapse are former colonies, or countries annexed by major empires such as the USSR, is easily explained. In Europe the modern state has evolved over centuries, starting 800 years ago with the Norman state in Sicily that was later ruled by the Hohenstaufen Emperor Frederick II. In Africa this state was simply superimposed on the traditional tribal cultures as an instrument of foreign domination. The borders of these states were drawn up as colonial interests dictated. In most cases it was a matter of demarcating the spheres of influence of European states. The affected populations were not consulted. They received this state as their dowry when they were released, after the Second World War, into an independence more or less real.

The border issue pinpoints one weakness of these states. Often the same tribes are living on both sides of the state border, with the same language and traditions: and they are living together in the same state with completely different tribes. Why this has to be so remains a taboo subject, because any attempt to correct at one point what the colonial powers settled with a ruler is bound to undermine the stability of the entire state structure.

A second weakness usually lay in the fact that the rulers had a different understanding of their state than the one acquired over time by French presidents or Swedish kings. Whoever was in power was not obliged to attend solely to the common good, but looked upon the state as his private sinecure, which had to produce a decent return. Not everyone took it to the same lengths as Mobutu Sese Seko of Zaire, who, when he smilingly confessed to a German government minister: *"Vous savez, je suis capitaliste!"*, did not mean that he subscribed to free-market principles, but was saying instead: this Congo is my private enterprise, from which, as a good capitalist, I extract my profit, and as big a profit as possible. No wonder that the towns in this state starved after Mobutu's departure, because the roads had deteriorated to such an extent that supplies of food could not be brought in from the surrounding countryside.

What Mobutu, backed by the US for decades as a loyal ally in the Cold War, took to excessive lengths in the vast expanses of the Congo, found more moderate expression in what sociologists call "rent seeking". Ulrich Menzel has given a succinct account of this economic variant, which is neither a market economy nor a planned economy: "The basic income here comes not from labor (wages) or entrepreneurial activity (profit), but from political control of high-yield resources. Concessions for the exploitation of natural resources such as oil, minerals, diamonds, tropical forests or fishing grounds are granted to foreign companies in return for payment of a rent to the country's political masters. Such rents can also be extracted by imposing arbitrary taxes on foreign trade, allowing rusting tankers to sail under a flag of convenience, or permitting imports of toxic waste. They can also come from development aid, whether in the form of credits, project assistance or gifts. There are countless ways of siphoning money off or extracting payments, inventing 'transaction costs' by setting up bureaucratic hurdles that can only be got over by paying a bribe." (Ulrich Menzel, "Der Zerfall der postkolonialen Staaten", in: *Aus Politik und Zeitgeschichte*, Vol. 18-19/2001, p.3 ff.)

Reading this description of rent seeking, one is reminded of the warlords who use similar methods to acquire the money they need to keep their mercenaries on side. Except that they have no laws, no national flag and no national anthem, nor indeed a bureaucracy: just their armed mercenaries, who basically do what the smart gentlemen in their dark suits do in the capital, only in a much more direct and brutal way. So the distinction between warlord and minister is relative rather than absolute, both in fact and more especially in people's perceptions. If a government really does see its state differently – i.e. not as an instrument of personal enrichment – it has a hard job persuading others of this.

Where rent seeking is combined with dictatorial violence, where it has to be propped up and secured by lawless brutality, it prompts a violent reaction. Whether the violent opponents of a violent regime call themselves rebels, whether they draw support from ethnic or religious groups, whether they are criminal gangs or simply feed on the outrage provoked by those in power, they are no more and no less able to justify their violence than those who profit from rent seeking.

So the road that leads from a monopoly on the use of force to a market trading in violence, from state-authorized violence to privatized and commercialized violence, is not a long one: and where the powers of the state are used to enforce the economic interests of the rulers, that road is quickly travelled.

IV. The same road is even shorter, its destination even more certain, where governments attempt to outsource state-sponsored violence to paramilitaries or militias, who very quickly start to pursue their own interests and acquire a taste for a way of life where they can get with a gun in minutes what others take weeks to earn through honest toil.

The privatization of violence from above supplements, reinforces and legitimizes the privatization of violence from below, especially as paramilitaries rapidly adapt their methods to the normal practices of those they are sent to fight. They become self-serving agents trading in the market for violence that supersedes the state monopoly on the use of force.

Whatever the fine gentlemen in the capital can do, the warlords and paramilitaries can do in the provinces. So at least the world appears in their eyes. In the eyes of the people on the receiving end, any difference presumably lies in what their current rulers can offer them. If the government provides piped water, medaled roads, clean hospitals, and possibly even judges who cannot be corrupted, the men and women in the villages will refuse their allegiance to the warlords for as long as possible. But if they see in their government only personal avarice pursued by state means, they will settle for an evil which, if not lesser, at least does not appear to be greater. The chaos in the Congo must have come about in much this way.

To put it in more formal, academic language: a state is robust enough to protect itself against collapse and disintegration when it is perceived not just as an apparatus of power and violence that serves selfish interests, but as a set of rules, "with the aid of which public benefits such as domestic peace, certainty of the law, infrastructure, a functioning monetary system or an education and health system are provided". (Ulrich Menzel, "Der Zerfall der postkolonialen Staaten", in: *Aus Politik und Zeitgeschichte*, Vol. 18-19/2001, p.4)

V. This also explains why it is so much easier to wreck and destroy a state than to build it up again. To bring about its collapse, it is sufficient that it ceases to provide – either because it is too poor or because it is too corrupt – vital public services: so no more impartial judges, no protection against crime, no schools, and no clinics where a doctor or a nurse can put a broken arm in a splint. Once criminal gangs or the mercenaries of warlords are able to maintain their reign of violence unchallenged, it becomes virtually impossible to make good what has previously been neglected. The local potentates will not tolerate any state-appointed judges, policemen, teachers or doctors. They will not tolerate the provision of public services by the state, even if they have neither the intention nor the capacity to deliver those services themselves.

Since no investor will expose his money to the risks that are inevitable in a stateless environment, the *entité chaotique* descends into a downward economic spiral that makes humanitarian aid as necessary as it is problematic. For the warlords will only admit such aid if they can cream off something for themselves. So anyone who wants to help the defenseless poor must pay off their tormentors, which only adds to the chaos.

For the most part the international community is pretty helpless when faced with a collapsing state. It is too late for development aid. Europeans and Americans have little appetite for sending their troops into a dangerous and chaotic unknown, and if neighboring states send their troops in, they may readily adopt the methods and practices that have become normal there. This is why the collapse of a state takes only years, while the rebuilding of a state can take generations.

It is therefore hard to understand why so little attention is paid to what Menzel calls "the crumbling of the post-colonial state as such" – and how little political activity it engenders. People talk of "failed states", states that have not passed their examination, as it were, just as one speaks of poorer and richer states, and they talk of "failing states", without devising any strategies for preventing "failing states" from quickly becoming "failed states" for the duration. These failed states are simply written off by the big concerns. It is not possible to do business there, they have no purchasing power, and they are not needed. They are superfluous. But what seems superfluous in economic terms can become extremely dangerous politically. If one state after another starts to implode in Africa – including once stable states such as the Ivory Coast – the result could be waves of migration that Europe will not be able to keep out. Do we not constantly hear it said in the US that failed states all too easily become breeding grounds for terror? That makes sense, not least because there can be no law-breakers in a territory without laws. In a place where nobody claims a state monopoly on the use of force, terrorists are left undisturbed to train their fighters along military lines.

VI. But why did the phenomenon of state collapse and disintegration become so prevalent in the 1990s, continuing unabated into the first decade of the new century? Here again there are undoubtedly many different reasons at work. But there are three that probably matter more than the others.

First, the distance in time from the colonial era. When colonies became independent states in the 1950s and 60s, hopes rose on a tide of euphoria. Now that the decisions were no longer taken in Paris, London, Brussels, Rome or Lisbon, things were bound to improve fast. Disillusionment quickly set in. As far as the infrastructure, railways, roads, hospitals and schools are concerned, many of these young states are still living today off what they inherited back then. And quite a few of them have now exhausted that inheritance.

What is also exhausted in many cases is the hope of better times to come, and the faith in people who promised, and continue to promise, those better times. Added to this is a growing awareness of the arbitrary nature of state boundaries. Where, in a state like Nigeria, with the largest population in Africa, Muslim fundamentalism meets a powerful Christian minority, which in some states of the federal republic constitutes a majority, not only is the unity of the state as a whole under threat, but so is its monopoly on the use of force.

More important is the second reason: the end of the Cold War. What was thought of, at the time of the Cold War, as the "Third

World", i.e. a world that was not linked to one side or the other by formal alliances, was nevertheless – or for that very reason – another battleground for the global struggle. Unofficially most states had made their choice, most of them in favor of the West. Neither side, East or West, was interested in how government was conducted in these countries: all they cared about was dependable support, not least when it came to voting in the UN. If a government was regarded as anti-communist, it was not only supported by the West through development aid, but the presiding dictator could also count on assistance from the secret services, especially the CIA. If on the other hand a government had loudly proclaimed its "socialism", it was inundated with aid and declarations of friendship from the Soviet Union and its allies. Internal conflicts were discouraged and limited by the fact that they were immediately seen in terms of the larger East versus West conflict – even if they did not fit the pattern. So a so-called "communist" rebellion in West Africa would have stood as little chance as a "counter-revolutionary" uprising in Cuba. Even up until the mid-1970s the West avoided challenging the Portuguese colonial rule in Angola and Mozambique – suspecting those who did seek to challenge it of dubious motives – because the Portuguese were members of NATO, whereas nobody knew what path a free Mozambique or Angola would pursue.

In short, the two Cold War adversaries were a force for stability wherever their writ ran, and they had the means to ensure that stable conditions prevailed. With the collapse of the communist world, that interest quickly disappeared. A despot like Mobutu now seemed unnecessary and an embarrassment, so he had to go, along with a number of lesser figures. Now nobody could rely any more on borrowed stability: all that counted was the home-grown variety. And in most cases the outlook was not good.

VII. Almost simultaneously with this shock, the neoliberal version of globalization began to take effect. This is the third, and possibly most important reason for the decline of the state.

When the gospel of liberalization, deregulation and privatization is proclaimed in the Western industrial nations, this can trigger all kinds of developments that are generally regarded as sensible, such as the dismantling of pointless bureaucracy. The state in Europe is not as overweight as neoliberal critics would have us believe: but nor is it so weak that it cannot survive a couple of years of slimming. It is different in the countries of the southern hemisphere, which are called "developing countries" even when there is virtually no economic development there at all. As far as Europe is concerned, nobody had the power to prescribe such treatments from without, but it was a different story in Africa and Asia. Countries that needed aid from the World Bank and credit from the International Monetary Fund – both of them based in Washington – had to accept the conditions that the IMF in particular was able to dictate. For a long time these conditions were not the result of careful study of the countries in question, but simply followed the pattern laid down in the Washington Consensus. If liberalization, deregulation and privatization were the right thing to do economically, then they must be the right thing to do everywhere. If the minimal state was the only right option, then this must be true across the board, even in places where the state was already wasting away.

And so the IMF prescribed and imposed its programs of structural adjustment, which always amounted to the same thing: devaluation of the currency as an incentive to export, and thereby to earn the foreign exchange that would at least pay the interest on the crushing burden of debt; reduction of the national budget and cutbacks in public expenditure, including spending on education, health, and above all welfare – social security being out of the question anyway. Of course, the proliferation of bureaucracy is a problem that afflicted, and continues to afflict, poor countries too. It is the consequence of a "clientelism" that is hard for modern Europeans to understand – the fact that ministers and senior government officials have to take care of a clientele made up of their extended family and tribe. But the budget cutbacks led in many instances to cuts in the salaries of middle-ranking and junior officials – salaries that were hardly generous to start with.

Corruption was endemic in Africa and Latin America long before the IMF adjustment programs came along. But these programs increased the number of states in which the additional earnings from corruption were essential if an official was to feed his family and other dependents. Corruption, which is where state collapse always begins, was factored in as an additional source of income when setting salary levels. Corruption, also in the form of bribes, became an essential part of the system.

Besides, savings were made by cutting precisely those services that differentiated the state from the warlords: education, health, and care for the needy. Whatever the economic effects of such measures might have been – and generally they failed to deliver in their turn – they served to weaken a state that was already weak to start with. Repressive and largely uncontrolled violence: this was what the warlords had to offer too, who had made a business out of violence. What the hard-working women in particular wanted and hoped for from their state, the state increasingly failed to provide.

VIII. Did the powerful advisers who put the emaciated state on a starvation diet know what they were doing? Martin Shaw (*Theory of the Global State*, Cambridge 2000) thinks this probable: "For liberal and free-market globalizers the perceived undermining of state power has generally been not only inescapable, but a good thing." (ibid., p.260) Many, one should probably add, have subsequently learned a thing or two from the collapse of states.

Critics like Stiglitz complained early on that the IMF was forcing states to "submit to the neoliberal catalogue of norms to the point of self-sacrifice". And he was right. Some of those states no longer exist – including huge states like the Congo.

Now Europe is gradually waking up as well. At the Munich Conference on Security Policy, Germany's Federal President Horst Köhler urged security policy makers on both sides of the Atlantic to drastically increase levels of development aid. Köhler told *Die Zeit* what was troubling him: "If Africa descends into chaos, if the Africans do not get a fair chance, it will delegitimize globalization." (*Die Zeit* No.50/2004, p.6)

Köhler knows what he is talking about. He was the first – and for a long time the last – German to head the International Monetary Fund. But he must then explain why, if what he says is true, he exchanged the top job at the IMF for the office of German Federal President. At the IMF he was in one of the very few positions where he could influence the decisions that actually determine whether or not "Africa descends into chaos". As German Federal President he can utter warnings. That is not a little: but it is a lot less.

Can we learn something from the phenomenon of state collapse, which evidence suggests is by no means confined to Africa and Central Asia? At the very least it raises questions that are worth reflecting on:

1. If the state falls apart at the point where it can no longer provide the public services that citizens are entitled to expect, and to which they also have a right, what then is the minimum that the state has to provide?
2. If the cause of such a fatal failure is the lack of moral fiber (corruption) and the absence of adequate financial resources, should it be left to economists to decide how that moral fiber is to be sustained or renewed, and how the necessary finance can be procured?
3. If the erosion of the state monopoly on the use of force through the privatization and commercialization of violence is so closely related to the collapse of the state in developing countries that the one drives the other, and both appear at times to be two sides of the same coin, does this also apply to the industrial nations?
4. Is the minimal state propagated by the neoliberals actually viable? Or is it just a theoretical construct?

5. Should a society leave it to economists to decide what constitutes the duty and responsibility of a state?

IX. People generally learn to appreciate the true value of a commodity only when they no longer have it. We learn the value of our daily bread only when we are forced to go hungry. We find out what freedom is worth when we have lost it. And people discover the value of the state when they have to get by without it.

Where the state has withered away, the law of the jungle prevails. Strength lies in having access to weapons, and having some idea how to use them. This is much easier today than it was a hundred years ago. This is why children with submachine guns can become mass murderers. Often they become child soldiers, so that they are no longer numbered among the helpless who are exposed to foreign violence. Armed children are an invention of privatized violence. There are more of them today than the total number of men and women serving in the German *Bundeswehr*. Where there is no state to make and enforce laws, it is the women who suffer the most. Exposed to sexual violence, they wear themselves out trying to support their children. Whatever they manage to grow to feed their family they can lose at any time to marauding mercenaries, who either steal the crops or simply destroy them. If they resist, they risk being killed. In the end they decide that any state is better for them than no state at all.

Many Iraqis, especially Iraqi women, must have felt the same when the mob started looting after the American invasion, and the occupying forces just stood by and watched. Where the state disintegrates or is simply abolished by the victor, power passes to the boldest, the most brutal and the most ruthless.

A monopoly on the use of force wielded by a despot can be broken in a matter of days, as the Iraq war shows. The resulting vacuum may be state-free, but it is not power-free and most definitely not violence-free. And once this vacuum is filled by privatized violence, it may take decades before a new, non-despotic monopoly on the use of force can be established.

The state is an institution invented by men for the purpose of subjugating violence to the rule of law and regulating human social existence, including amongst other things – but only amongst other things – their economies and markets. Men have experimented with their invention, often with devastating consequences. But now they think they know what kind of state is needed to subjugate all forms of violence, including state-authorized violence, to the rule of law. This institution is vulnerable and transitory, like man himself. If it becomes sick and weak, it needs skilled doctors to take care of it.

Perhaps we really can "drown the state in the bathtub", as Grover Norquist recommends. But once it dies such a death, nobody can revive it. The best that can be hoped for then is the emergence of a new state, protected and nurtured by the international community. It takes a long time for it to grow up and stand on its own two feet. And, let it be said for the benefit of Norquist, who might find this argument more persuasive: an awful lot of money.

The state is not endlessly resilient. It is not a cat, which always lands on its feet whichever way one throws it. Nor is it, as many believe, a weed, which, while it cannot be entirely eradicated, nevertheless can and should be kept under control by the gardener, so that there is enough space and light for the stuff that is grown for sale: flowers, and above all cauliflowers. Modern chemicals allow us to eradicate everything that is deemed to be a weed. The only trouble is, lots of other things die in the process – things that we need in order to live.

Chapter 8

Threats to Liberty

I. Vigilance is the price of liberty. This is one of the lessons that Europeans draw from their history. If one asks against whom this vigilance needs to be directed, the answer given by most people at the start of the 21st century is unequivocally "against the state", or more precisely, against its tendency to become too powerful, all-powerful, and to suppress liberty. This has to do with the experiences of the 20th century, certainly, but it remains true in every age. As long as states exist, their citizens will need to remain vigilant lest the power of the state be abused, and the instruments of state power be used to curtail or suppress liberty instead of promoting and protecting it.

The only question is whether it is sensible to focus solely on this danger, and overlook others in consequence. It might well be that in the 21st century there are dangers out there that could pose a more immediate threat to us, at least here in Europe, than the danger of excessive state power.

Wherever Europeans fear for their liberty, we can expect to hear the name George Orwell invoked – in the 21st century as in the 20th. In an essay entitled "Fight the Matrix", which appeared in the British newspaper *Guardian* of 5 June 2003, Timothy Garton Ash writes as follows: "In Orwell's centenary year, the 'war against terrorism' takes us to an Orwellian world in a quite unexpected way. We are told that Oceania (America, Britain and Australia) must go to war against Iraq, or, as it might be, Orwell's Eastasia or Eurasia, on the basis of reports from secret intelligence sources."

Responsibility for this war rests in the first instance with two politicians, of course, George W. Bush and Tony Blair: and clearly Garton Ash, as a Briton, is having a go at his own Prime Minister.

But these politicians could not blur the boundary between reality and fiction all by themselves. For that the media has to help out, not the state-owned media, public broadcasting institutions, but private media concerns, who have their own agenda. The only effective resistance came from the BBC. As Garton Ash writes: "The broader point is that 21st century democratic politics operates in a media world of virtual reality, in which appearance is more important than reality. The genre of modern politics is neither fact nor fiction, but faction. It is a 24/7 drama documentary. This is the world not of Newspeak but of Newscorp. It is shaped not by a single totalitarian bureaucracy, but by an intimate, habitual interplay between politicians, spin doctors, PR consultants and journalists working for media corporations."

Who does not remember the world of CNN in the months following 11 September 2001, which consisted almost entirely of the "war against terrorism"? They were not telling lies; intelligence reports, as a rule at least, were vetted for reliability, as is right and proper; and people differentiated between fact and supposition. And yet it all served to create the very view of the world that Bush needed for his Iraq war. There were no simplistic claims that Saddam Hussein and Osama Bin Laden were in league with one another. The news editors at CNN knew very well that the two were deadly enemies. But of course the statements of the

President and his ministers were broadcast repeatedly, round the clock. Garton Ash writes: "Yet the trend, in journalism as in politics, and probably now in the political use of intelligence, is away from the facts and towards a neo-Orwellian world of manufactured reality. This is something slightly different from (though close to) straight lies." It is the world in which, when Bush was re-elected in November 2004, half the American population still believed that Saddam Hussein, the Iraqi dictator, was preparing to deploy weapons of mass destruction and – worse still – make them available to Al-Qaida.

Of course, this "manufactured reality" is not confined to the foreign policy sphere. It also makes a lottery of domestic politics, as when the British tabloid *The Sun* announces that if Blair signs up to the European Constitution, two million British jobs will be lost.

In any event, the real danger comes not from "the state", but from media moguls obsessed with circulation figures and market share. Here is Garton Ash again: "The best place to start combating neo-Orwellianism is at the end of the food chain, in the media. So if you want to fight the Matrix, become a journalist. Find the facts and report them. Like Orwell." What Garton Ash does not talk about are the interests of those who hire journalists and pay their salaries. What if they want very different journalists from Garton Ash or Orwell?

When Orwell talked about journalists, he meant people who wrote for newspapers, perhaps also for radio stations. But these two media, newspapers and radio, now have a diminishing impact on public opinion, which is dominated by television. Most Bush voters in the mid-West do not read newspapers. They sit in front of the TV and want to be entertained. The television stations out there – privately owned, of course – are in the hands of people who are interested first and foremost in making money, tend to be Republican supporters, are very comfortable with the neoliberal hegemony and are receptive to neoconservative populism, especially when it is dressed up as patriotism. Naturally they have nothing against those "values" which fundamentalist preachers forge into political weapons. And they find it edifying when an American President presents himself as God's champion battling the forces of evil. Now try and imagine the journalist George Orwell working for such a TV station...

II. In the matter of newspaper readership the Italians are more like the Americans than their neighbors in central or northern Europe. Their consumption of daily newspapers is 119 per thousand of the population, far lower than in Great Britain, Germany, Scandinavia, or indeed France. At the same time Italians watch an average of 4.5 hours of television a day, putting them in the top league for Europe. Newspapers are something for the politically interested minority, who also watch the state-owned RAI television channels. Italians with little interest in politics do not read newspapers and tend to avoid the state-owned television. They are well served by the three private channels of Mediaset, which belong to the empire of Silvio Berlusconi. Otherwise there is virtually nothing, with state-owned television and Mediaset sharing 90 per cent of the television audience. This is what is termed a "duopoly".

For many years Silvio Berlusconi was also one of those who had no desire to wrestle with politics, parties and programs. His friendship with the dubious Bettino Craxi, then Italy's Prime Minister, does not imply any political sympathies – for Craxi's party, the Socialists, or anyone else. What it does show is that Berlusconi understood very well how economic power and political power can each make use of the other, and how the collaboration can make both parties more powerful, and above all richer.

Berlusconi was, and still is, an entrepreneur before all else. He started out in the construction industry. In Milan, where he was born in 1936, he built the satellite town Milano Due. He then set up the town's own television system called Telemilano. Over the years this evolved into an effective monopoly over private television in Italy. Here Bettino Craxi proved very helpful. As private television was not regulated by law, Craxi legalized it –

temporarily – by decree, while at the same time ensuring that the Italian parliament did not pass any laws that would have interfered with his friend's business dealings. Berlusconi used this unregulated breathing space to build up a monopoly in the medium that was soon to become more important than all the others put together.

In addition to three television channels Berlusconi's Fininvest empire has since acquired department stores, supermarkets, Italy's largest publishing house, the top-selling TV guide, cinema chains, financial services, even telephone books – not to mention a football club, the famous AC Milan.

This is not the place to discuss the events that accompanied Berlusconi's rapid rise. Whether, where and in what way the successful entrepreneur broke the law, whether and how the Italian justice system has succeeded in calling him to account, is of interest to us only in so far as this subsequently gave rise to a conflict between the executive and the judiciary that is without parallel in any democratic state.

What concerns us here is how Berlusconi the entrepreneur turned his economic power into political power, and how he then used this political power to secure his economic power, particularly the power of his media empire. But we shall also see what a pitiful role the Italian state played in all this, and continues to play to this day. How could a big-time entrepreneur become Prime Minister of his country without relinquishing his monopoly control of privately-owned television? And how could the legislature connive at giving this Prime Minister immunity from criminal prosecution?

III. Throughout the Cold War Italy's christian democrats were a guarantee for the West, and in particular for the US, that the Italian Communist Party (PCI), the largest communist party in the Western world, would not come to power. This meant that no government was conceivable without christian democrats, even if, on occasion, the government was not actually led by a christian democrat. So Giulio Andreotti was Prime Minister seven times, and held various ministerial posts on 33 occasions in the meantime. It was always the same old people: they just kept swapping roles.

Although governments were constantly changing, there was no time pressure. What one government left unfinished, the next government could take up. If their interests diverged too much, nothing at all happened. This explains why there were no relevant laws in place when Berlusconi set about building up his private television empire and dominating the market. The arrangement he came to with his friend Craxi went unnoticed in an environment rife with nepotism and corruption, which are hard to avoid when a party is allowed to see itself as irreplaceable and irremovable. There were rumors, of course. But nothing much came of it.

It was only after the disintegration of the Soviet Union, when the filler of anti-communism was crumbling, that a few courageous state prosecutors toppled the entire party system in a matter of months. The official christian democrat party splintered into small groups, or disappeared into the political no man's land. The communists, who had long since gone their own democratic way, now rebranded themselves as the "Democratic Left", which led to a split with the dogmatic Marxist-Leninists. The Left remained a functioning political force, while in the centre and on the right a vacuum was created.

The fact that new forces now rushed into this vacuum and filled it up was a necessary and normal democratic process. The fact that a big-time entrepreneur forked out a few million in the process is not exactly textbook democracy, but it is not unusual, and provided the payments are disclosed, it is legal here and in other countries. But now something unusual occurred in Italy.

At the beginning of 1994 Berlusconi announced on Canale 5, the most respected of his TV channels, that while he had no intention of going into politics himself, he was in favor of a coalition movement that would enable a helpless majority to arrest the victorious advance of a well-organized minority, namely the Democratic Left. And so Forza Italia was born. It was not a party that is organized from the bottom up, nor was it one that under German law could have put up candidates for election to parliament. There was no time for that anyway. Forza Italia was an election machine built up by Berlusconi's Fininvest business empire, and in particular his Publitalia advertising agency. Formally it consisted of a network of loosely affiliated clubs, which were not subject to any laws governing political parties. By mid-February 1994 there were already 13,000 such clubs, with a combined membership of around one million.

When the government resigned on 13 January 1994, it was the signal for the start of an election campaign on all Fininvest media outlets for a political party that did not actually exist as yet. On 26 January Berlusconi announced his candidature. Nobody had put his name forward, because the party that could have done so did not yet exist. But he now decided who could stand as a candidate for Forza Italia. Where he had no knowledge of specific individuals, his employees at Fininvest and Publitalia were assigned to gather the necessary information.

As early as January 1994, when Berlusconi announced his decision to found a political party, he had added: "30 per cent of the electorate already support us." Coming from the man who ruled over private television, this claim was believed. The fears that haunt the founders of political parties in Germany, faced with the 5 per cent hurdle, have never troubled him. Even Italy's state-owned television based its allocation of broadcasting time on the estimated 30 per cent share of the vote. This is the kind of thing that party founders everywhere dream of.

IV. Italy's state-owned television is structured quite differently from public service broadcasting in Germany. When there is a change of government in Berlin following a general election, this has no immediate impact at all on the ARD and the ZDF. The directors of the individual regional TV stations (*Westdeutscher*

Rundfunk, Mitteldeutscher Rundfunk, etc.) stay in post, because they are entirely independent of the federal government, likewise the joint spokesman for the "Association of German Public Service Broadcasters" (ARD). Only in the supervisory bodies of the ZDF are there some minor personnel changes, not significant enough to create new majorities.

In Italy the RAI channels are officially subject to the Italian parliament, which fills the five seats on the Governing Board with three representatives of the ruling coalition and two representatives of the opposition. The Governing Board's first duty is to appoint the RAI Director-General. This is decided by a simple majority, so commonly by a vote of 3:2.

At the time of the 1994 election Italy's state-owned television, which had to try and maintain its neutrality, at least when it came to allocating airtime for party political broadcasts, was certainly not on Berlusconi's side. And his first period of office, lasting seven months, was not long enough to push through radical changes here. But it was a different story following the second election victory of his coalition in 2001. By a majority of 3:2 a supporter of Berlusconi became President of the Governing Board, and another, Agostino Saccá, was appointed Director-General. This is not to say, of course, that the Prime Minister had the same direct access to the RAI stations that he had to the Fininvest channels. But at the very least he was able to prevent public service television acting as a counterbalance to his privately owned channels. The kind of harsh, not to say devastating criticism that every German government has to expect, not least from commentators on the ARD or ZDF channels, is something that Berlusconi no longer had to fear from the medium that is by far the most powerful in his country. How is such a thing possible in one of the founding member states of the European Union?

When, far too late, the Italian parliament finally moved in 1990 to enact legislation aimed at bringing a degree of order into the media market, Berlusconi had already grown so strong that nobody dared to take him on any more. The new law with the cute name *legge Mammi* resembles a suit of clothes made to measure for the media czar. Despite all its complicated provisions, the law sanctioned the licensing of all three Berlusconi-owned channels in 1992, until in December 1994 – after the elections, therefore – Italy's Constitutional Court declared the *legge Mammi* to be null and void, on the grounds that it had simply served to protect and legalize the position of power held by Fininvest.

After Berlusconi's first defeat, many people in Italy and elsewhere thought that the *Ulivo* government of Romano Prodi would now devote all its energies to passing a law that made it impossible for anyone to amass both media power and political power. They tried, and the opposition accused them right there of "unfairly attempting to influence the market". But what the Italian Left managed to salvage of the *legge Maccanico* in 1997 had virtually no impact on the duopoly in the Italian television industry. What has survived is principally the *Autoritá per le garanzie delle communicazione*, a board of eight persons chosen by the relevant parliamentary committees. The *Autoritá* has wide-ranging powers, and can even propose new legislation. What it actually achieves depends on who sits on the board. And as long as Forza Italia has got a majority representation, the board would not take any action that hurts Berlusconi.

There is now a law known as *par condicio* which seeks to establish equal conditions for all in elections, in particular equal access to the electronic media. But for one thing the exercise of media power is not confined to elections. More dangerous is the creation of world views, hierarchies of values, which can then be appealed to, or simply called up, in an election campaign. And for another thing a large business concern is not deterred by fines of the kind that the *Autoritá* can impose.

V. Berlusconi's media power was obviously a campaign issue. Most Italians could see that the country's Prime Minister should not own the most important medium of public control. So Berlusconi promised that in the event of his election victory he would "resolve" the conflict of interest between political power and media power within 100 days. What was meant by this rather vague formulation could be seen from the draft law that his minister Franco Frattini brought before parliament, which was quickly accepted by the majority in February 2002 – so within the 100-day time limit. This law did indeed stipulate that a member of the government could not, amongst other things, own any mass media outlets. But once again there was a *punto salva Berlusconi*, whereby "non-executive owners" who are not involved in any way with decisions taken by the governing bodies are exempted from this provision. As the name "Berlusconi" did not appear in Mediaset's organization chart, there was no conflict of interest. So he was not affected by the legislation. In other words, the problem was simply made to go away by some terminological sleight of hand. Berlusconi's election promise was formally fulfilled, but in reality it was broken.

Many observers of the Italian scene believe that Berlusconi did not, as he claimed, enter politics in 1994 in order to save Italy from communism (which was already starting to crumble), but to safeguard his media empire – which would have been seriously at risk if the Left had won a big majority. Whether or not this was his principal objective, he achieved it. The political power that he obtained with the aid of his media power served in turn to buttress his media power.

Once a person has combined political power with media power, he can do something that no politician in a mature democracy can dare to do: he can fight the legal system. If a government minister in France or Germany is under investigation by the state prosecutor, he has to resign, even if the head of government is convinced of his innocence. Berlusconi can respond to every accusation and every charge by abusing the judiciary. These state prosecutors, and often the judges too, are simply dismissed as communists or the tools of communists. They are not interested in justice or the law: they are only interested in bringing down the man who saved Italy from communism. Just imagine a head of government in Britain,

Holland or Germany calling the independence of the judiciary into question in this way. The media from all parts of the political spectrum would unite in hounding him out of office. But this is not the case in Italy. The core of state authority is the judiciary. When the head of the executive can systematically vilify the judiciary, the state is in a bad way. As is the law, which it is the state's duty to protect and enforce.

Imagine if a French government minister or even the Prime Minister himself were due to go on trial accused of falsifying financial records. And then the government uses its parliamentary majority to have the offence of falsifying financial records removed from the criminal code, or to get the length of the statutory period of limitation reduced to the point where a conviction is no longer possible. For how long, for how many days, could such a government survive?

VI. This is not an argument about who are the better democrats – the British, the Germans or the Italians. The subject of this book is the state. Does the state pose a threat to freedom only when it is too powerful – or also when it is too weak? The Italian state was too weak. It was too weak, as Martin Morini has shown, to deal with the Mafia. (Martin Morini, "Historischer Kompromiss: Berlusconi und die Mafia", in: *Blätter für deutsche und internationale Politik*, No.3/2005, p.311 ff.) The christian democrat governments sought an accommodation with the Mafia back in their day. After a few years of *mani pulite* (clean hands), Berlusconi has reinstated this tacit arrangement.

It is bound to end in tears when the state controls the entire economy, when state power and economic power are in the same hands: so said the critics of the system that called itself socialist, and was run by communist parties. This was plain enough even to those who had not, like Berlusconi, imbibed anti-communism from the cradle. It is not good for the state to take control of the economy.

But is it any better for the economy to take control of the state? Better if a successful entrepreneur, who has already acquired supermarkets, cinema chains and publishing houses, then takes over Italy plc? And this in the firm belief that the best thing that could happen to Italy would be for him to run it as he runs his companies? Is it better for the state if this entrepreneur then comes to an arrangement with other enterprises, including the Mafia?

When Helmut Schmidt called himself Chairman of the Board of Germany plc, it was, as was noted earlier, a gesture of modesty, if perhaps a misguided one. In Berlusconi's case similar remarks were a sign of hubris and obtuseness. He really does think the state was a service provider for the economy, and that it must be run like that. In complete contrast to Schmidt, Berlusconi despises, indeed hates the state. He hates the state prosecutors and judges who do not know how a businessman has to earn his money, and who, instead of cowering reverentially before the successful entrepreneur, just get in his way with their ridiculous legal niceties. He hates and despises the legislators who begrudge him his media empire, an empire that he has built up by his own efforts, and which none of these bigoted nay-sayers would ever have been able to create. He hates the state which, unlike a business concern, subjects every power, and the power of the government in particular, to more and more checks and controls. Berlusconi hates the state that he has to run – and wants to run. He hates it because it is so completely different from a business enterprise, and because – as he must surely have realized in the meantime – it cannot be turned into one.

As a card-carrying neoliberal he does not want to drown the state in the bathtub, but he does want to cut it down to size, reduce it to what the economy needs. So he is always in favor of tax cuts. But at the same time he is responsible for a national budget, and has to stay within the 3 per cent deficit limit in order to keep the EU Commission off his back.

VII. The state simply cannot be privatized. It can be used, as Berlusconi has demonstrated to an astonished Europe, to serve the private interests of a head of government – even to the extent of enacting legislation – if that head of government has sufficient control over the media. But there are limits, if only because in Europe, at least, there is no eradicating the idea that the state is somehow bound up with the common good.

We can learn important things from the chaotic Italian experience. Economic power and political power both hinge on the media. And increasingly, though it varies from country to country, that means television. Whoever controls television is able to influence our values, our view of the world, the way we live, and what we regard as important or pressing, or conversely as unimportant, trivial or harmful. If money and sex are the only things that sustain the viewing figures, television is the ideal breeding ground for *homo oeconomicus*. And all these things can then be played upon for political ends. Which is exactly what Berlusconi has done. Others can do it too. They do not need to own the television channels: it is sufficient for the politicians to ally themselves with the owners.

Among the institutions that have stood the test of time in the Federal Republic of Germany – human fallibility notwithstanding – is public-service broadcasting. It is not a state broadcasting organization, but nor is it a private broadcaster. All the relevant social groups have their part to play. It is structured in such a way – and this differs slightly from one federal *Land* to another – that it would be very difficult to turn it into a tool for someone's – anyone's – personal use.

So it must be cause for alarm – and not only in Germany – when the European Commission challenges this arrangement, on the grounds that television is a form of service delivery. Entertainment and information are commodities, it is argued, and the normal regulations governing competition must apply, which rule out state subsidies – including, therefore, license fees levied by the state. The ZDF's legal adviser, Carl-Eugen Eberle, summarized the clash of views succinctly when he said that the EU was engaged in reinterpreting "the German concept of broadcasting freedom with a public-service orientation" in favor of "the right of the individual to engage in economic activity". That is a polite way of putting it. Nobody is "reinterpreting" anything here: what they are doing is viewing culture as an economic activity pure and simple, and putting a value on it accordingly. And considerations of public service do not figure in this kind of thinking.

So the argument about public-service broadcasting in Germany is likely to show whether Europe is still capable of standing up for its own traditions, which hold that culture, while not taking place in a money-free zone, is not on that account a commodity. This is the battleground on which will be decided what in Europe belongs to the market, what is the business of the state, and what is a matter for civil society. And these decisions will also show whether Europe has understood the Berlusconi phenomenon. What it teaches us is that freedom is at risk when the state falls prey to private interests. For then the state can no longer do what it is obliged to do under every European constitution: protect and safeguard freedom, including – and especially – against the all-too-powerful.

Chapter 9

The Market, Civil Society and the State

I. As the 21st century began, there was much talk of civil society, little if any mention of the state, while the market was busily competing with both to control more and more areas of our lives. The key instruments of that control, privatization and deregulation, were discussed above in Chapter 5.

There were good reasons why it was suddenly "modern", perhaps even fashionable, to get behind the idea of civil society. The danger that the all-conquering market might lead us into a market society where everything was treated and traded as a commodity was now too obvious to overlook. But the entrenched skepticism vis-à-vis the state would not yet permit any discussion of where the state should set limits on the market. So people focused instead on civil society, of which one could at least be sure that it was neither a market nor a state.

Otherwise much remained unclear. Sociologist Helmut Dubiel (writing, for example, in the German newspaper *Frankfurter Rundschau* of 23 June 2001, p.7) attributed this to the fact that some people talked about civil society as though it were a present reality, while others presented it as a utopian vision. The confusion arose from the fact "that civil societies are either seen as an empirical sociological phenomenon, which assumes tangible form in clubs, political associations, lay organizations, social movements, networks, self-help initiatives, neighborhood contacts, the so-called "third sector", etc. Or else civil society is understood as a utopian ideal, as a regulative idea, whose pure normativity sheds a critical light on the corruption of everyday life."

It follows from this, presumably, that the "corruption of everyday life" emanates from the market, but also from the state – or more precisely, from the agents of the market and the state. To counter their malign influence, something better, more humane, more wholesome is needed.

That Dubiel himself does not quite see it that way emerges from the four threats to civil society that he lists, of which the fourth and most radical – barbarism – is the one that interests us most. "The fourth and last form of the uncivil society is barbarism. The term is used here in the sense of the complete breakdown of a society's moral and legal order, its reversion, so to speak, to a state of nature. We can find immediate contemporary examples of this fundamental type of uncivil society in the societies of Africa, south-east Europe, and in the southern territories of the former Soviet Union, where the structure of the state has imploded as a result of civil wars."

The radically uncivil, barbaric society comes into being where the state has ceased to exist. Dubiel elaborates: "In these societies the state's legitimate monopoly on the use of force, which in its most reduced form would consist of an intact chain of military command, has been replaced by the natural state of warfare between tribes and gangs and the virtual collapse of all social functional systems. Such conditions of barbarism are furthest removed from civil society. 'Barbarism' is the antithesis of 'civil' society."

II. But if the totally uncivil society and its barbarism are the product of state collapse, then there must be a positive correlation between civil society and the state. From time to time Europeans have to be reminded of this by non-Europeans. A case in point occurred during a round table discussion at a government conference on the theme of civil society on 2/3 June 2000 in Berlin.

It was a South African academic in the study group on civil society who contradicted the European delegates when they argued that the state and civil society are at opposite ends of a seesaw: when the state is up, civil society must be down, and where civil society is strong, only a lean, not to say thin, state is necessary. It is not like that in the countries of the southern hemisphere, objected the African academic. Only where there is a functioning state, a state monopoly on the use of force based on the law, the judiciary and the police, together with a minimum of state social policy, can a civil society thrive. In conditions of political chaos, she argued, it stood no chance at all. And conversely: only where this civil society is alive and well can the state perform its tasks effectively over the long-term. In short, the state and civil society need each other, argued the expert from South Africa: they can only go forward together – or fall apart together.

Certainly she speaks from an African perspective. But the same applies for the whole of Africa and for many countries in Asia and Latin America. In a broad strip stretching from the northern border of Namibia to the southern border of Egypt, there are no functioning states or civil societies. The state as connecting link between economic and military power, between money and gun barrels, simply does not exist. Weapons can be bought, mercenaries recruited – and hired out – taxes can be collected, even in the absence of laws. What remains is the rule of the Kalashnikov over an extremely uncivil society.

Europe, especially Western Europe, is not Africa. But we can learn from the Africans nonetheless. In Russia the state is weak because there is no civil society, and civil society cannot grow because the state is weak and the Mafia too powerful. Those who question Vladimir Putin's democratic credentials need to understand that Putin has to rule a Russia like this – and not Holland or Switzerland.

The government conference in Berlin revolved around the functions of the market, civil society and state institutions. All three are essential for a democracy, none can or should take on the responsibilities of the others, and none is sustainable in the long-term without the other two. The communist attempt to replace the market with state chains of command was a failure. The neoliberal penchant for replacing politics with the market at every opportunity is likewise doomed to failure. Even the most vibrant civil society does not render the legislature and the executive superfluous, and even the best organized state needs civil society if it is to remain true to the values of European democracy. We need an alliance between the "transnational" state and an internationally connected civil society.

III. In one important respect the state and civil society both stand in direct opposition to the market: in both, the state and civil society, politics is practiced. Politics is not just about the struggle for power – and power struggles do take place in clubs, editorial offices, action campaign groups and churches: invariably politics is **also** about how people live and how they very emphatically (in most cases) **do not** want to live. Civil society is the most original instrument that people use in order to be able to live the way they want to live. We look to civil society, as we look to state institutions, to satisfy needs that the market cannot meet. To that extent civil society is likewise a locus of political activity.

Civil society can ease the burden on legislators and governments, it can spur them to action, push them forward or hold them back. But it can never replace them. It is good that private schools exist alongside state schools. But without state funding (up to 90 per cent), most of them would not be viable. It is good that grants and scholarships are also offered by charitable foundations. But there will never be enough for all students, and what charitable foundations are able to do is governed by tax legislation anyway. It is good that clubs and churches concern themselves with the welfare of families. But whether or not children put too much strain on the family finances is decided by MPs in parliament.

Non-state organizations, or non-governmental organizations – NGOs – as the Americans call them, are necessary and helpful, even when, as in Seattle, they disrupt an international conference. But whether, if left to their own devices, they would create a flourishing world economic order, is open to question. For that they doubtless lack more than democratic legitimacy.

It was already apparent back then, in the year 2000, that anyone who backs and supports and champions civil society is going to get into a discussion about what the state should provide in the way of services (including services for civil society), in what areas the state is irreplaceable, and what the state could look like if it is able to depend on a vigorous civil society. If civil society cannot replace the state, how can the two give each other mutual support and encouragement? How can they become partners?

Former President of the European Commission Jacques Delors doubtless meant something similar when he spoke of the European model. By that he means a Europe in which the market does what it is the market's business to do, and civil society does what committed citizens feel able to do, and in which the organs of the state establish a framework for both – a legal, social and ecological framework. He means a Europe in which the non-commodifiable never becomes a commodity. And this can only succeed where the state and civil society enter into a partnership of mutual respect.

After his own experience of the totalitarian state, SPD politician Adolf Arndt suggested that the democratic state must become like a dress for society: not tight and restrictive, but a good comfortable fit, allowing and encouraging free movement, but also protecting the wearer against wind, rain and cold, as well as providing warmth in the winter. It is even in order for this dress to be a little on the pretty side, so that others are moved to inquire about the dressmaker. This would be the activating state, without which civil society cannot thrive, but which is constantly being challenged, criticized, preserved from sclerosis and humanized by forces within civil society.

That the time has come for a public debate on the subject is shown by a remark made by Michael Sommer, president of the German Trade Unions' Federation. This thoughtful trade unionist, who discovers the limits of his power every day, said to the *Süddeutsche Zeitung* (No.16/2005): "We need to stop doing politics hand to mouth, and ask ourselves two key questions: what should the state be doing for us in the 21st century? And how are we going to pay for it?"

IV. There are functions that are assigned by common consent to the market, the state or civil society. Few will dispute that the production and distribution of bicycles and vacuum cleaners is a matter for the market, and that the conviction of criminals is a matter for the state. And it is pretty clear that the care of the dying, as undertaken by the hospice movement, is better handled by civil society than by the market or the state: imagine a "Care of the Dying plc" or a "Department for the Care of the Dying". But much of what was accepted by common consent 20 years ago is now the subject of argument. And those who feel a sense of political responsibility need to decide where they stand.

The monopoly on the use of force that is constitutive of the state is not negotiable or up for grabs. Likewise the justice system, police, army and penal system. Just as there cannot be a private justice system, so neither the police, the military nor the penal system can be entrusted to the market. If a business wishes to hire in security to protect its premises, it should be free to do so, provided the security companies operate under the overall control of the police. If people sleep more soundly knowing that their house is guarded by a private agency, they should be free to buy such additional protection. But they should not be allowed to set off the cost against tax. For by doing so they would be depriving the state of the money it needs to ensure that their neighbors can sleep soundly too. Whether the canteen in an army barracks is run by a non-commissioned officer (NCO) or by an outside contractor is purely a question of what works best. But the bearing of arms must be restricted to those who are authorized by law to do so.

A democratic constitutional state in Europe should not tolerate no-go areas or gated communities. It should not stand by while criminal gangs mark out their territories on the periphery of big cities, nor should it allow the rich to exclude themselves from society and hire their own private police force. And if the state has lost the strength – and the means – to impose its will, then politicians must see that it gets them back again. That is what politicians are for.

V. It gets a lot more difficult when we turn to matters of culture and science. The state is very definitely not responsible for the truth, but it is responsible for creating the conditions in which truth can be pursued. In the case of the natural sciences, the distinction is very clear. The state's job is to facilitate the business of research: whether a particular research finding is correct and valid is a matter for the scientific community to decide. The state can only enter the picture again when the application of research findings is up for discussion.

It gets more complicated with the humanities. What constitutes historical truth cannot be established by legislation or by a majority ruling. Holocaust denial is forbidden not because the historical facts are clear, but because such denial insults the victims and their descendants. The role of the law is not to establish historical truth – which is not subject to legislation – but to protect people who are in need of protection.

When the German parliamentary Committee of Enquiry on German National Policy between 1949 and 1989 was preparing its findings and the then majority sought to establish where the government's policy had been right and where it had been wrong, it quickly became clear that these were not matters that could be resolved by politicians. Historical perspectives are not decided by a vote of parliament: they are formed in the course of academic debate between historians. And many aspects will remain forever contentious. Which is why, incidentally, it is by no means clear that an authority such as the Federal Commissioners for the Records of the East German State Security Service should be publishing its own series of "scientific monographs", now running to over two dozen titles, which address themselves to such general topics as *The Place of 17 June 1953 in German History* – and this under the title *The Repressed Revolution* (2004). An authority charged by law with the administration of *Stasi* files is not qualified to pronounce on historical truth. Not that it would be any more qualified if a rather less one-sided and controversial view of things were being promoted with taxpayers' money. By all means let a government agency examine its own history. Nobody minds if the foreign office commissions historians to write a history of the foreign office. But it is not the job of the German Foreign Office to write a history of German foreign policy.

What is the job of the state, though – and in Germany that means the regional or *Land* governments – is to fund departments of history in our universities, even if, unlike departments of chemistry, they do not contribute directly to the country's economic competitiveness. The state is not in the business of imposing a view of history, whether official or semi-official: but it is responsible for ensuring that a view of history can emerge from the discourse of historians. The reason is simple: no human society can survive unless it engages with its own history. So with the destruction of language in Orwell's *Nineteen Eighty-Four* comes also the destruction of the collective historical memory.

The state as envisaged and predicated by the European Union has no official state philosophy. And yet the state is responsible for ensuring that philosophical thought can continue to thrive on the basis of a rich philosophical tradition. The state does not have the right to establish an approved literary canon, but it does have a duty to facilitate the academic study of literature. Literary critics may suggest their own lists, others are entitled to reject them, but education ministries are only allowed to decide what should be tested in the school-leaving examination. It is no coincidence that the important literary prizes in Germany are not awarded by the state, but by groups within civil society. In the case of the Peace Prize awarded by the German Booksellers' Association, commercial interests happily coincide with the judgment of civil society.

VI. Wherever culture is under threat at the start of the 21st century, it is not the state that intervenes but the market. The state cuts a sorry figure in this regard, not because it wants to do too much, or because it interferes where it has no business, but because it does too little, or to be more precise: because it is no longer capable of discharging its responsibilities.

One can of course, like the World Trade Organization (WTO), view cultural assets as commodities, which are in competition with each other and therefore should not be subsidized. This would mean that the only music that can be played is the kind that makes enough money at the box office to pay the musicians a decent salary. That would spell the end of all symphony orchestras. So there would be nobody left who could play the symphonies of Mozart, Beethoven or Brahms, while the symphonies of Gustav Mahler would never have become known, and perhaps never even composed. And commercial sponsorship is not the answer either. A major orchestra needs continuity and the ability to plan ahead with confidence; it cannot get by for long by lurching from one donation to the next. Quite apart from the fact that opera houses and concert halls have traditionally been built and maintained with public money. Who is going to take on that role in the future? The end result would probably be that opera – and not just opera – would be ousted and replaced by the musical. A large part of our musical culture would simply die out.

Are the local-authority music schools unnecessary? Do they just keep prices artificially low? Or are they the expression and mainstay of a musical culture which, while enacted predominantly within civil society, in music clubs, church choirs and jazz bands, would nonetheless wither away without state assistance? When Germany's regional governments sponsor competitions for young violinists or pianists, when they fund regional youth orchestras, or provide the grant aid that is necessary to make music festivals possible, they are acting in ways that are normal and necessary in civilized nations. This is why UNESCO, the UN's cultural organization, is seeking agreement on a form of words that can be invoked by individual nations to defend themselves against interference in cultural matters by the WTO. If the WTO and UNESCO fall out, perhaps the nations in question will win the freedom to act in accordance with their own political culture.

What it means for the culture of a country when it is abandoned to market forces can be seen from the programming put out by private TV channels. No amount of self-regulation can alter the fact that decisions about what is aired and what is not are governed entirely by the viewing figures. The diversity that was once promised by the champions of privatization has turned into an endless diet of the same old thing: game shows with big prizes, shock reality shows, crime and sex, all strung together by mindless babble. The fact that the public-service broadcasting corporations have gone further down the same road than their charter allows is not an argument for abolishing them, but rather for strengthening their remit.

The nation that has fought hardest, and probably with the greatest success, against the surrender of culture to market forces is France. To begin with it demanded an *exception culturelle*. Now the talk is of a *diversité culturelle* and the need to save it. That is only possible, argue the French, if the state retains the right to sponsor, subsidize and set quotas. In the United States, on the other hand, subsidies are seen as an imposition on consumer freedom, dictating the choices that consumers make. It is depressing that these differences of opinion between Europe and the US are hardly ever addressed in our media, and that only a handful of people are even aware of them. The outcome is not unimportant after all, both for European culture and for the future of the state. A state that is not allowed to support cultural activities, that must stand by helplessly while our culture is impoverished and trivialized: would that not be, for many Europeans, a ridiculous institution?

VII. The collapse of communism must have finally made it clear to everyone that the state is well advised not to interfere unnecessarily in the economy. The planned economy may still work in a country with only three factories. But only the market can cope with the complexity of a modern, globalized economy.

For as long as markets have existed, it has been necessary to clarify what is permitted in them and what is not. Every market needs a legal framework. This is established by the state through its laws. This framework grows more complicated as the economy becomes more complex. Special areas of expertise emerge, such as stock company law, competition law. Those intent on wholesale deregulation of the market should ask themselves what a meeting of shareholders would be like without any legally established procedures.

While the legal framework is there to ensure that business can be transacted in an orderly fashion, that suppliers and buyers know what the ground rules are and how far they can go to protect their interests, the social framework seeks to prevent people and their labor from becoming just another commodity. If the legal framework safeguards the functioning of the market, the social framework protects the human dignity of those who offer their labor for hire.

Responsibility for the social framework does not rest exclusively with the state. In most European countries the issues of working hours, working conditions, vacation time and in particular the level of remuneration are determined through negotiation between employers and trade unions. This is a laborious process full of potential for conflict: but the deal that the tired negotiators on both sides finally put before the public after exhausting all-night meetings is generally not only more likely to hold up than anything that government ministries could devise, but it also has the support of a broad majority on both sides. So the state is well advised to guarantee freedom of association in the constitution, and to let the contracting parties sort things out between them where they can.

This does presuppose that the two sides are reasonably well balanced. That balance can be disrupted when, for example – as in the early 1970s – the order books are full, the labor market is cleaned out, and employers are more fearful than usual of strikes. And conversely when, as has been the case since the mid-1990s, there are millions out of work who would gladly agree to all kinds of concessions if it meant finding a job. Add to that the fact that business owners can threaten at any time to shift production and shut down whole plants, and the borderline between diktat and negotiation becomes very fluid.

At which point the cry goes up for the state to intervene and restore the just society that nationally organized trade unions can no longer force globally operating capital to deliver. But what happens when powerless trade unions appeal to a government that is no less powerless?

VIII. When the Constitutive Assembly drafted Article 20 of the German constitution in 1949 – "The Federal Republic of Germany is a democratic and social federal state" – there was no heated debate about the meaning of "social". The importance of social engagement was self-evident in a land that had been destroyed and bled dry, in which many were at last able to eat their fill again after years of starvation rations. It was necessary to balance the needs of those who had been forced from their homeland against the needs of those who had remained; of those who had been bombed out of their homes against those who had escaped the bombing; of those who survived the war intact against those who came out of it crippled. Nor was the Constitutional Court, which derived the principle of the welfare state from Article 20, in any doubt as to the social responsibility of the new state. Article 20, after all, is one of those whose contents cannot be amended, even by a two-thirds majority.

Since then the wind has changed. Now the debate is not just about **how** the welfare state can deliver, but about **whether** it should. Wolfgang Kersting, a professor of philosophy in Kiel, concludes that "even a limited redistribution of wealth by the welfare state places restrictions on the civil right of the individual to dispose freely of the fruits of his own labor". (Wolfgang Kersting, *Theorie der sozialen Gerechtigkeit*, Stuttgart 2000, p.1) This is not the place to ask how the good professor would argue if the regional government for Kiel decided that a minimal state could dispense with the odd chair of philosophy, and duly consigned him to that state of involuntary redundancy in which millions discover that nobody wants their labor, and that without "a limited redistribution of wealth by the welfare state" they are condemned to starve. And not because they do not want to work, but because they are not allowed to work.

Kersting is not alone in his views. It has become commonplace to declare social security a private matter – or, if the state does get involved, to label it a threat to freedom. And now this kind of thinking has spread into the wider political arena – far beyond the small party that turned its back on the welfare state in 1996 with its "Karlsruhe Bill for a Liberal Civic Society".

IX. Anything that can be said on the subject was said a hundred years ago, by a liberal politician who has given his name to a foundation closely associated with the FDP: Friedrich Naumann. Even back then there were liberals who thought that unrestricted freedom of contract was the answer to everything. The laborer can enter into a contract to sell his labor, rent an apartment, buy insurance. What more does he want? Naumann, who expressed himself in plain and unpretentious language, offered them food for thought: "Old-style liberalism said: you are all free, for you can trade freely with all that is yours, including your labor. Consequently the laborer can sell his labor for the best price he can get, and if he does not like the price, he will not sell. If he is expected to work in premises that he finds too vaporous and cramped, he will decline to do so, for he is a free man! But we now know – and they could not quite see this at the time – that the only free man is the man who knows where his next month's wages are coming from. If he does not know that, then the finest theory about how free we are to sell ourselves is no help to him." (Friedrich Naumann, *Die politischen Parteien*, Berlin 1910, p.92 ff.)

Unrestricted freedom of contract, as the legal scholar Otto von Gierke knew even before Naumann, puts the weak at the mercy of the strong. For Naumann or Gierke, much of what calls itself "neoliberal" today would rate as old-school liberalism. And Naumann knew that social security, far from diminishing or jeopardizing freedom, is what makes real freedom possible for the majority of people. To those old-school liberals he would have objected: what use is it to me if I claim, or indeed am entitled to, the undiminished fruits of my labors, if nobody wants the work I do? If I am made redundant not because my employers cannot make the business pay, but because they want to increase their return on capital?

Journalist Heribert Prantl, writing in the *Süddeutsche Zeitung* of 27/28 March 2004, similarly felt himself transported back to the 19th century: "When inequality exceeds certain limits, it becomes a form of servitude. The risk of this is greater now than it was 150 years ago – and it is the job of the state to prevent that risk from arising. To that extent the right to social justice is the right of our citizens to expect action on the part of the state to avert excessive inequality by appropriate means."

Social justice – unlike, say, the right to freedom of expression – cannot be enforced by going to court. It is, as jurists say, not a subjective right but an objective principle, and one to which the German Federal Republic pledged itself in its constitution. There never can be and there never will be a set of circumstances that is judged by everyone to be socially just. But most people have a reliable instinct for what is manifestly unjust. The expression "screaming injustice" reminds us that excessive inequality is enough to make people scream. And sometimes they do more than scream. Here is Prantl again: "Inequality must not exceed certain limits. The right to social justice means establishing those limits, drawing a line, and charging the state with putting measures in place to ensure that it is not overstepped."

Unlike the contemporaries of Friedrich Naumann, we now know what can happen if the state fails to draw that line, either because it does not want to, or because it is too weak to do so. It forfeits the loyalty of a majority of its citizens. And if it was already in a fragile condition before, it now goes into terminal decline.

X. We are familiar now with a further function of the state of which the generation of Friedrich Naumann and Max Weber could know nothing: the establishment of an environmental framework.

When the UN Commission chaired by the Norwegian Gro Harlem Brundtland published its report in 1987 calling for sustainable development, this call was linked to a conclusion that was as simple as it was revolutionary: what we had hitherto understood as "development", the rapid industrialization of the northern hemisphere and the attempts by the south to catch up – all this was suddenly "not sustainable". The German term is *nachhaltig*, which first appeared in 1713 in a treatise on forestry, and it described a forest management regime whereby no more timber was felled than could be replaced by new growth. In other words, we were living off our – environmental – capital, and there was no way that this could go on indefinitely. But the "not sustainable" verdict implied more. The continuation of a form of "development" that released more and more greenhouse gases into the atmosphere each year, that sealed more and more of the countryside under concrete, and continued to poison the soil, was not possible. It would end up choking on its own excrement.

Turning around non-sustainable development and making it sustainable requires action on the part of the state. Markets are geared to short-term profit opportunities: that is their strength and also their weakness. If there is more money to be made from bloated gas-guzzlers than from a car that returns 60 mpg, the motor industry will produce what it can sell most profitably. The fuel-saving small car will be bought by motorists when fuel gets a lot more expensive, and when the road tax on eco-friendly vehicles is dramatically reduced. Even better would be to tax consumption by transferring the road tax to the fuel – though all attempts to do so in Germany for the last 30 years have failed because the tax on fuel goes to the Federal government and road tax goes to the *Land* government. But the point is this: to make sustainable what is currently unsustainable requires the intervention of the state with its laws and regulations. The state needs to promote combined heat and power technologies because they make the most efficient use of energy sources; the state needs to subsidize renewables so that it pays householders to install photovoltaic panels on their roofs. And in its agricultural policy the state must encourage forms of husbandry that retain the natural fertility of the soil and protect the groundwater from nitrate pollution. And so on.

The crucial point for the purpose of our present discussion is that the market is not equipped to deal with the challenge of sustainability – not unless the state creates the conditions which ensure that what is sustainable is also profitable. Certainly civil society also has a part to play here, and it is active in countless associations and cooperatives. But it depends on legislation by the state – such as the German Law on Renewable Energy – to create opportunities for successful action.

XI. Perhaps our descendants will view it as a savage irony of history that at the very moment when scientists became clear about the state's entirely new and unarguable responsibility for turning around non-sustainable development and making it sustainable, an ideology denouncing everything that was now palpably necessary as a sin against the market began to carry all before it.

Hence the hysterical campaigns against the environmental tax – which nobody now cares to be reminded of. Hence the mindless refusal of the US government to sign up to the Kyoto Protocol. Hence the incessant whingeing of those who want to get rid of the environmental framework – in so far as it has been established in the face of so much opposition – as part of a radical program of deregulation.

In the meantime scientists and politicians have come to understand that ecological sustainability is not the only thing we lack. We are realizing that neither our social welfare systems nor our public finances nor our development policy are fit for the future, to say nothing of the *Bundeswehr*, as bequeathed to us by the Cold War. In the meantime we now have a debate about whether our democracy is sustainable or not, whether it is compatible with a globalized, radicalized capitalism as interpreted by neoliberal doctrine; and many are concerned accordingly for the future viability of the democratic state. That concern is the subject of this book.

This is not the place to announce remedies. But before remedies of any kind can be drawn up, discussed, voted on and implemented, we need to be clear about one thing: if we wish to make sustainable something that, if simply left to the market, would lead to disasters of a greater or lesser magnitude, then we need political engagement – an engagement that draws its strength, certainly, from civil society, but which has to use the means and resources of a fully functioning state. In short: if it is the case that sustainability can be taken for granted less today than at any time in history, then the future of our children and grandchildren depends more than ever on a state that is capable of effective action.

If the state had not existed at the end of the 20th century, it would have been necessary to invent it, at the very moment when an outmoded ideology began to disparage and denigrate the state that was already there – happily – even if it was, like all the works of man, highly imperfect. And worse still, began to starve it to death.

Chapter 10

The State and Values

I. At the beginning of the 18th century, during the reign of
Frederick William I, a mixed population of Germans, Poles,
Masurians and Kasubians coexisted harmoniously in Prussia,
with the addition of Frenchmen in the capital Berlin and
Dutchmen in Potsdam. Some were Lutherans, others were
Catholics, others again belonged to the Reformed Church. They
did not yet constitute what Johann Gottfried Herder, some
decades later, would call a "people" (*Volk*), but they were
beginning to think of themselves as Prussians. What bound them
together was not ethnicity or religion, nor did they yet feel
themselves, like the French in 1789, to be a nation, a community
of will made up of people who stood for values like liberty,
equality and fraternity. They were subjects of the King of Prussia,
who by rights should have called himself only "King **in** Prussia".
From the middle of the 18th century onwards they were Prussians
because they felt a loyalty to the state whose first servant the
brilliant and ruthless Frederick II had declared himself to be. It

was the state itself that brought them together, and from which they took their political identity. Nor did this only apply to the ruling class of Junkers.

This state, in which someone like Voltaire could seek refuge, constituted a value in itself: many were proud to belong to this state, to serve it, to promote its welfare. To be a Prussian meant to be upright, incorruptible, dutiful, to think and act for the benefit of the common good, to uphold law and order, and to tolerate differences of language or religion. Values shaped the state, the state in turn shaped those values. A Prussian patriot was anyone who rendered signal service to the Prussian state. And it was in Berlin that Professor Hegel from Swabia defined the state as "the embodiment of the moral idea".

The many Poles who came to Prussia, particularly after 1772 as a result of the partitions, did not feel out of place there – until Prussia became the leading power of a new German Empire in 1871. At which point, against a background of rising nationalism, they no longer belonged. They were able to think of themselves as good Prussians, but not as Germans.

What bound the Germans together from Lake Constance to the Baltic was not a shared state but an Emperor, and above all a national sentiment that quickly degenerated into nationalism. Bavaria, Prussia and Württemberg were separate states with their own monarchs, their own legal systems, their own administrations and their own anthems. Even in the First World War there were no German regiments as such, only large numbers of Prussian regiments and others from Baden or Saxony. Only the Navy was an Imperial enterprise.

The German national state, in legal terms an association of states, an alliance of princes, was given the name "German Empire" (*Reich*). This harked back to the "Holy Roman Empire of the German Nation", on which the sun had set two generations earlier. This Holy Roman Empire, which saw itself as heir to the *Imperium Romanum*, was not a state, but a kind of wrapper holding together a whole collection of states. But it was perceived as something consecrated, hallowed – almost like the secular arm of Christianity. Thus Burgundian Frenchmen could feel as much at home in this imperium as Bohemian Czechs. And what the Germans came to associate with the term "German Empire" after 1871 was not so much a specific state as an idea, something consecrated and – if a good few sermons from the First World War are to be believed – something hallowed too. From the Holy Roman Empire to the patriotic hymn "Holy Fatherland in distress, Your sons to your defense do press" is not such a long way as the four intervening generations might lead one to suppose. Now it was no longer – as in Prussia – the state that united and motivated people, but nationalism, linked to the idea of the *Reich*. One could be a Bavarian patriot, despise the Prussians, and yet see oneself as the most loyal upholder of the imperial idea.

In retrospect, from a distance of 130 years, it seems only logical that Otto von Bismarck should have branded his domestic political opponents – the Catholic Centre Party, the left-wing liberals and increasingly the early social democrats too – not as enemies of the state, but as enemies of the *Reich*. They all obeyed the laws of the state, after all, the regional *Land* laws and the laws of the *Reich*. But there was good reason to doubt whether they approved of the nationalistic reinterpretation and rededication of the imperial idea.

II. German nationalism was less closely tied to the state than its French counterpart. The French nationalist was proud of his state, with its capital Paris, which the nation had struggled and fought to create through revolutionary action. The German nationalist, on the other hand, could be a loyal servant of the King of Württemberg who looked with suspicion on Berlin. Or a Silesian businessman who revered the head of the house of Hohenzollern as the King of Prussia first, and only then as the German *Kaiser*.

The opposite of the "enemy of the *Reich*" was therefore not the patriot, but the "nationally minded citizen". A patriot – self-styled or so called by others – is someone who is willing to serve his *patria* selflessly. In the Middle Ages this *patria* could well be a free imperial city or a minor principality. The "nationally minded" landowner could exact protective duties on corn which benefited him but harmed the community at large, as long as he demonstrated the right national attitude of mind – by calling his seasonal laborers *Polacks*, for example. Later, in the 1930s, it was even possible to show one's national attitude of mind by flouting the laws of the state.

In retrospect the German catastrophe could be seen coming in August 1932, when Hitler, already the leader of the strongest party in the *Reichstag*, proclaimed his solidarity with the five SA men who on the night of 9 August had kicked a young communist to death in front of his own mother in the Upper Silesian village of Potempa, and were now in jail awaiting trial. What was surprising was not that the *Führer* sided with murderers, but that the public reaction was either mixed or non-existent. Where were the churches and the jurists, who should have publicly declared: "Anyone who seeks to annul the right and duty of the state to punish murderers should never hold public office!" Instead of which, *Reichskanzler* Hitler released the murderers from jail less than a year later.

There have been nationalistic excesses in France, too, such as the Dreyfus Affair. There too the course of justice was perverted, and it took far too long before the – manifestly innocent – officer was rehabilitated. But amidst all the turmoil of this shameful dispute, one thing was clear to both parties: if Dreyfus is guilty of treason he must be punished, but if the Jewish army captain is innocent, he must be acquitted and rehabilitated. Nobody dared to question that the laws of the French Republic must apply. But this is exactly what Hitler did in 1932. And only a small portion of the German public even noticed what this signified. There is a big difference between a nationalism where pride in the rule of law is part of the emotional mix, and one where the rule of law is seen simply as an obstacle, whose removal is in the national interest.

The last legacy of that division of the nation by the founders of the *Reich*, of that exclusion of the "enemies of the *Reich*" by the "nationally minded", are the arguments that periodically flare up on the subject of patriotism. Many politicians seriously believe that one is a patriot if one can utter the words "I love my country", and that anyone who finds this difficult is an "unpatriotic scoundrel". Many even think, like the "nationally minded" in their day, that the definition of a good patriot is someone who regards most of his countrymen as bad patriots. Using patriotism as a stick to beat people with rapidly leads to absurdity.

III. Jürgen Habermas was also familiar with these mechanisms when he took up the idea of "constitutional patriotism", which German philosopher Dolf Sternberger had brought up for discussion back in the 1950s. But what is a "constitutional patriot"?

Is he someone who can recite the constitution by heart? Is he supposed to meditate each morning, not on the "Word for the Day" like the Moravian Brethren, but on an article of the constitution? Is a constitutional patriot someone who can cite an article of the constitution in support of any wish or demand he cares to make? Is it someone who scents breaches of the constitution everywhere? Or just someone who makes a fine speech on Constitution Day? Someone who regards the constitution as so perfect that he refuses to countenance any amendments? Or even someone who regards his own constitution as superior to those of other countries? One can dismiss such questions as merely frivolous. And of course they miss the point that Jürgen Habermas was trying to make. But in a country where serious men and women, including politicians, can believe that one becomes a patriot by denying the patriotism of others, one must reckon with grotesque misunderstandings.

Laughable as these questions are, the fact remains: what is at stake here is the constitution of a country, in this case the Federal Republic of Germany. The constitution exists for the benefit of the state. It is the "basic" or "fundamental law" (*Grundgesetz*), which determines what the state looks like, how it will function, and also – and this is important – what is its purpose, what it is **for**. Consequently anyone who extols the constitution necessarily finds himself talking about the state.

IV. A constitution is first and foremost a set of procedural ground rules for the organs of state, which thereby become constitutional organs: parliament, which in Germany also includes the second chamber, the *Bundesrat*; the federal government; the federal Constitutional Court. Their respective powers have to be defined, the lines of demarcation carefully drawn. These lines may stand the test of time or they may not. The requirement in Germany's Basic Law (Article 67) that a Federal Chancellor can only be voted out of office by electing a new one (constructive vote of no confidence) has proved workable, the establishment of a clear distinction between the powers of the *Bundestag* and those of the *Bundesrat*, less so. This is why a Federalism Commission was set up. The establishment of a Constitutional Court (Article 94) has proved to be the right decision, even though the Court, like all constitutional organs, has a tendency to expand its own powers at the expense of others – the Federal government and the *Bundestag* – as in its rulings on tax law. This is no reason to question the need for its existence, but no reason either to applaud its every judgment.

So the constitution, like the state that it seeks to bring about, is the work of fallible humans, more especially humans who cannot possibly know what will be necessary and right thirty or fifty years down the road. Consequently the constitution needs to be constantly adapted to changing exigencies.

Now one can regard such ground rules as a good thing, successful and effective, and one can argue that they should be perpetuated. But is this an adequate foundation on which to build patriotism? Surely the other, value-related side of the constitution is more appropriate for that?

A document like Germany's Basic Law that places an obligation on the state, in its very first Article, to respect and protect human dignity is more than just a protocol for a value-free apparatus. Similarly imbued with an awareness of values are the first 19 Articles, which deal with the basic rights of the citizen. This is not mere political star-gazing. This part of the constitution is inalterable in its essence, and the basic rights listed here are legally enforceable. They "shall bind the legislature, the executive, and the judiciary as directly applicable law" (Article 1, Paragraph 3). Our task here is not to interpret the basic rights one by one, from the "Freedom of faith, conscience, and creed "(Article 4) to "Occupational freedom" (Article 12). Our task is to see how these things relate to an awareness of values and a hierarchy of values on which the new state was founded.

V. Basic rights are not the same thing as basic values. But they do relate to basic values. They only make it into a constitution if the fathers and mothers of that constitution believe in basic values that they want to see respected in real life. The many rights relating to different kinds of freedom are in Germany's Basic Law because freedom was a basic value for all those who helped to draft the text. Equality before the law (Article 3) and the prohibition on discrimination (Article 3, Paragraph 3) are elevated to constitutional status because its authors wanted the second principle of the French Revolution – *égalité* – to apply in Germany too. And when in Article 14 property is "guaranteed", with the additional proviso (Paragraph 2) that "Property entails obligations. Its use shall also serve the public good", this tells us nothing at all about the nature of those obligations. But it is a riposte to those who would claim it entails no obligations at all, apart from the obligation to amass more and more of it in perpetuity. The principle of social justice is not established or explained in Article 14: it is simply presupposed.

If we look for the values that underlie the constitution, we can also find them in places where the Basic Law does not lay down any basic rights, but merely rules on questions of procedure and areas of jurisdiction. The division of powers between the executive, the legislature and the judiciary is designed to safeguard freedom. The independence of the judiciary is designed to ensure that justice is done. The controlled redistribution of financial revenues between the individual *Länder* (Article 107: "Financial equalization") is an expression of the belief that the principle of solidarity should apply to the *Länder* too: the richer *Länder* should help the poorer ones. There is no mention in the constitution of such redistribution distorting competition between the *Länder*.

The value system underlying the Basic Law reflects the fact that no state can survive without such a value system. A state has to make laws. Not everything that seems morally right should be enshrined in law. But where there are no moral standards, the law is left dangling in mid-air. The state could not have made failure to render assistance in an emergency a punishable offence unless its citizens tended to the belief that people should help each other wherever possible and wherever necessary. Perhaps this particular section of the Criminal Code is a distant echo of the New Testament injunction: "Bear ye one another's burdens." But it would be utterly intolerable if the laws of the land were to prescribe who must assist whom in what circumstances.

The fact that murder and manslaughter attract harsh punishment has to do with the value we place on human life, as the fifth commandment – "Thou shalt not kill" – also reminds us. But the state does not have to punish by law everything that could be morally interpreted as an act of killing. In the abortion debate there were quite a few MPs who shared the Catholic position that abortions should be stopped, even if this involved sacrifices. But they hesitated to translate their moral conviction into punitive sanctions imposed by the state. The resulting legislation characterizes acts as unlawful, but refrains from prescribing punishments. Here we can discern a state that understands and acknowledges its moral responsibility as clearly as it understands and acknowledges the limits of its own ability to make things happen. And this is a good thing. A state needs to know what is expected of it and what exceeds its capacity, what its proper tasks are and where its limitations lie.

Every legal system is based on an awareness of values. If this awareness changes, the legal system must be reformed. When we read in Germany's Basic Law today (Article 6, Paragraph 5): "Children born outside of marriage shall be provided by legislation with the same opportunities for physical and mental development and for their position in society as are enjoyed by those born within marriage", we are dealing with a provision that is a good deal younger than the Basic Law itself. What today we take for granted is the work of the Justice Minister in the 1966-1969 Grand Coalition and later Federal President, Gustav Heinemann, who pushed through the reform of the law on illegitimacy. Prior to that many people believed that the protection of marriage and the family, as provided for in Article 6, required that an illegitimate child must be seen as "not related" to its natural father in the eyes of the law.

VI. While the state could not exist without an awareness of values, it is required to remain neutral in matters pertaining to religion, philosophy and personal conviction. The state is not responsible for truth. At the same time it is required not only to permit religious freedom, but to protect it. Can these two things be reconciled?

The churches in the Federal Republic of Germany really do enjoy more freedom than they did under the *Kaiser*. The "Alliance between State and Church" conferred much prestige on the churches, and more especially on the clergy, but it also earned them hostility. The alienation of the working class was a more or less inevitable consequence of the alliance between the Protestant churches in particular and the ruling class. Furthermore, many monarchs were not content just to be the titular head of a national church. They also interfered, especially in matters relating to clerical appointments. This is no longer possible in a secular constitutional state – not unless it is expressly regulated by concordat.

The free church in a free state is now established as a model that satisfies both parties. The state welcomes the church's social work, which alleviates its own burden, and the churches have the ear of parliaments and governments. The churches speak their minds on political issues that affect them, without attempting to dictate policy. And political parties seek dialogue with the churches, without feeling constrained to say what the churches want to hear.

Perhaps this is only possible because the values that are enshrined in our constitution and in our legal system are overwhelmingly Christian in origin. It is just that the churches in the 19th century failed to notice this. "Liberty, equality, fraternity" were for them revolutionary, anti-Christian slogans. The bishops of all faiths forgot that it was Jesus of Nazareth who insisted that all men and women, whether slaves or masters, are equal in the sight of God, that it is hard for the rich, not the poor, to enter into the kingdom of heaven, that all of us are meant to see our neighbors as our brothers and sisters. Intent only on their own authority, the princes of the church did not want to admit that the founder of their religion had opened up new realms of freedom when he said to his followers that the Sabbath was made for man, not man for the Sabbath.

The churches have since come to realize how heavy-handed has been their assault on secularized Christianity. They know that the trinity of values proclaimed by the French Revolution has Christian roots, particularly in the form that is familiar to us today: freedom, justice and solidarity. On these three fundamental values democracy in Europe – the democratic constitutional welfare state – is founded. On this trinity is founded what Jacques Delors has called "the European model". And where all three values are in play, where freedom, justice and solidarity sustain and illuminate each other, there the future of Europe lies.

It is not necessary to justify or interpret this trinity of values in Christian terms. A Jew, a humanist or an atheist can do it without turning themselves inside out. Probably a Muslim can do it too. Whether the Muslims want to, and whether they can, will determine whether they can be successfully integrated into European societies. We, the non-Muslims, must ask them to try.

VII. Constitutional patriotism, then, is the perpetual striving to make of the state what the constitution has envisaged, to get it to the point where the constitution wants it to be, to give currency to the values on which the constitution is founded. It means not only making use of our basic rights, such as the right to freedom of expression, but more especially ensuring that others can make use of them too. Constitutional patriotism is highly sensitive on the issue of human dignity – one's own, certainly, but more especially that of others. Constitutional patriotism is touchy where abuses of power are concerned, but it does not take it amiss when the constitutional organs use the power that has been temporarily vested in them.

This also means, however, that constitutional patriots take an active interest in the state whose basic rules are laid down in the constitution; that they feel a responsibility for what happens in – and to – their state. Putting this in the context of the European nation-states, as preserved in the European Union, this might mean that these states are the first locus of their responsibility – not the only one, but the primary one. A German constitutional patriot would then be someone who has devoted a substantial amount of energy to making the second German democracy a success; who makes sure that the fathers and mothers of the constitution did not labor in vain. To put it in a nutshell: the object and purpose of constitutional patriotic action is not the constitution, which has been around for a long time, but the state, which this constitution seeks to bring about.

And driven not by some *petit-bourgeois* trust in the state – "the government will sort it out, those in charge will do something about it" – but by the confident belief that "we **are** the state, we its citizens. We make sure that the organs of state do what they are supposed to do, and leave well alone the things that do not concern them. We are perfectly capable of doing things without the state if we want to, and that is what we call civil society. But there is no way we will leave the state to public officials or politicians. We are responsible for both, for civil society and for the state. And we know very well what we can tackle without the state, and where the state, our state, is obliged to act."

This brings us close to what our French neighbors call *citoyenneté*. Most dictionaries translate this baldly as "citizenship". But *citoyenneté* also connotes a certain attitude, namely that of the *citoyenne* and *citoyen*, who use their rights to fulfill their responsibility for the state and society. When the term *citoyen* was coined in the 12th century, it meant a free citizen or peasant as opposed to a serf, living in bondage and dependency. The French Revolution then adopted the term as an honorary title, as distinct from *bourgeois*.

So *citoyenneté* also means a society of free men and women who promote the common good, who feel responsible for what happens in their town and their country, who speak out against anything that restricts freedom, mocks equality or betrays a lack of solidarity, but who are not content just to criticize, but want to be involved in making decisions and shaping policy.

So constitutional patriotism, in the sense not just of an attitude of mind but of an active engagement, is very close to the idea of *citoyenneté*. And a good thing too. For to the extent that the functions of the state are transferred to the European Union, the attention of the *citoyen* or constitutional patriot will need to be directed towards Europe. It is likely that *citoyenneté* will lend itself more readily to being Europeanized than constitutional patriotism. Spaniards, Czechs and Hungarians could probably relate more easily to that than to a concept that owes its origins in part to specifically German difficulties with a guilt-ridden history. Europe needs vigilant *citoyens*, who continue to think of themselves as Frenchmen, Germans or Poles, but for whom the future of a common Europe is no less important than the future of their native land; political men and women, who for the most part, while they have nothing against patriotism as such, do not aspire to the title of patriot.

VIII. Democratic constitutions, and in particular the catalogue of basic rights that goes with them, tell us that a state has to do with values, that while it cannot create values, it can foster and protect them. But it takes more than just rights and law for a state to function, and to survive and flourish over many years: it takes certain characteristics that for the past two and a half thousand years have been called "virtues" here in Europe. For the most part they can be traced back to the four cardinal virtues named by Saint Ambrose: fortitude, temperance, justice and prudence.

If it is true, as has been said, that state collapse begins with generalized corruption, then the state is dependent on the virtue of incorruptibility. And that has to do with justice. If it is true that obedience to the law cannot be enforced by the threat of punishment alone, then the democratic state needs citizens who are by nature law-abiding, including those who, at the same time, make use of their democratic opportunities to amend or abolish a controversial law. If the monopoly on the use of force constitutes the core of statehood, then the active, critical *citoyen* must strictly respect this monopoly, and if necessary allow himself to be carried away without resisting when the police have to break up a sit-down demonstration. This calls for the virtue of temperance. Temperance is needful in our everyday lives as well. Jochen Vogel, who has occasionally been criticized for his unswerving correctness, puts it thus in his conversations with Heribert Prantl: "One must not become totally buttoned up and emotionless. But one must control oneself. This has something to do with the virtue of moderation and temperance." (Hans Jochen Vogel, Heribert Prantl, *Politik und Anstand – Warum wir ohne Werte nicht leben können. H.J.Vogel im Gespräch mit H. Prantl*, Freiburg 2005, p.92)

If it remains the case that most people encounter the state in the guise of officialdom, then the state should expect these officials to treat its citizens in a polite and friendly manner. And if citizens judge an authority in part by how long it takes to grant planning permission, then perhaps the virtue of diligence is not to be despised either.

The objection that secondary virtues such as diligence, reliability, correctness can be abused, even for the purpose of running a concentration camp, is entirely reasonable, but ultimately misleading. What are democratic constitutions and democratic politics for, if not to prevent just such a thing from happening? Whether or not secondary virtues can be abused is a matter for political debate and decision. And in the event that the political process breaks down completely, Germany's Basic Law (Article 20, Paragraph 4) gives all citizens, including officials, the right to resist: "All Germans shall have the right to resist any person seeking to abolish this constitutional order." Within the constitutional order of the democratic and social federal state there are no concentration camps. And outside this constitutional order there is no obedience, no law-abidingness, not even a monopoly on the use of force.

IX. The democratic constitutional state is sustained primarily by virtues for which there is certainly no call under a dictatorship. These include civil or moral courage, a form of fortitude. Someone living in a democratic Europe who draws attention to environmental hazards twenty years before most of the media does not have to worry about the *Gestapo* ringing his doorbell at five o'clock in the morning; but there are plenty of other ways of making his life uncomfortable. Which is why political engagement still demands a certain amount of courage, if its purpose is not simply to serve one's own career. Where moral courage is thin on the ground, or even absent altogether, democratic politics becomes sterile, stale, repellent. But where loyalty to one's own party conflicts with one's own well-founded convictions on an issue, and moral courage brings this conflict out into the open, politics acquires a human face. No wonder that the more the christian socialist politician Horst Seehofer was cold-shouldered by his own party and the christian democrats in 2004, the more the majority of the German public took to him. In 2008, he became leader of his party and Premier of Bavaria.

Having the courage of one's own convictions is another form of moral courage – as Seehofer also demonstrated. An informed opinion on complex issues only comes from thorough study – and there are few areas of specialization where this is possible. Unless a politician has sound reasons for rejecting the findings of specialists, he must go along with those findings. This happens every day in parliamentary committees, not because the politicians lack backbone, but because there are limits to the information that any of us can absorb. But when a politician has arrived at certain principled beliefs after many years of studying his brief, he serves the common good by championing and defending those principles, if necessary at the cost of his own career. For in doing so he is helping others to see the bigger picture. In any dispute between political parties, tactical maneuvering inevitably plays a part. Whenever a politician who cannot be accused of grandstanding sticks up for his or her opinion, supporting it with plausible arguments, it becomes clearer what the real issues are. That was the case when another CSU politician, Peter Gauweiler, who is more at home on the right wing of his party, refused to endorse the war in Iraq on the grounds that he is a man of law and order, which includes international law: and this constitutes a breach of international law. His point was well made. Anyone who watched this maverick politician at work could see that this was not tactical maneuvering, or vanity, but adherence to principle. This kind of thing may irritate a political party, but it is good for the democratic state.

Moral courage and truth to one's own convictions are often so intertwined that it is hard to tell them apart. When Seehofer stubbornly refused to accept the health care premium, many people called this moral courage. He himself probably does not see it that way. He cannot do otherwise than carry on warning. He cannot surrender his conviction without surrendering his own self. The two things together, truth to one's own convictions and moral courage, serve to remind us constantly that what matters in a democratic state is the common good, not individual careers.

This is why the Federal Republic of Germany was well served by the surprising and unswerving refusal of the Schröder-Fischer government to support the war in Iraq. On the world stage, in that suddenly the Federal Republic was seen as an independent player – happily in accord with France; and on the domestic front, where its citizens watched while an unparalleled media campaign against the government collapsed, and the anguished "I am not convinced" of Germany's Foreign Minister at the Munich Security Conference came across as authentic, while the reasons put forward to justify a war that had long since been resolved upon turned out to be pretexts or lies. It is lessons such as these that sustain the life of a democracy.

X. *Citoyenneté* or constitutional patriotism do not preclude love of country. Who has not said, without a hint of hypocrisy, "I love this city" – which need not mean that one does not love another city just as much, perhaps a city far away. Why should one not be allowed to love a landscape, especially if one grew up there? Apart from which, there is such a thing as a feeling of being at home somewhere. Only intellectual snobs would make fun of people who say, "This is where I belong, this is where I grew up. People know me here, and I know them: here people understand my dialect, and I do not have to pretend – I can just be myself."

This feeling is probably all the more intense, the smaller the area to which it relates. When somebody "loves" a city, they are usually talking about selected parts of that city; when somebody "loves" the Black Forest, they usually mean either the more sparsely wooded southern reaches of the Black Forest, or the dark, rolling spruce forests of the northern Black Forest.

Is it possible to love a country when one only knows a very small part of it? Probably: plenty of people love Munich without having explored all its suburbs.

Above all, we can all say of ourselves, unapologetically: "Even if I were completely free to choose, even if I were not held here by countless ties that have grown up over the decades, I would still want to live here, in this country. This is my country, with all its virtues and all its flaws. This is where I belong, this is where I feel at home, or at least more at home than anywhere else." There is no reason to despise those who, for whatever reason, cannot say this of anywhere. But nor is there any reason to sneer at those who can. For those who feel this way also have respect for other people in other countries who feel the same. And if to that is added the insight: "Here more than anywhere I feel responsible for what is happening and for what ought to happen", then the link is forged between the concept of *citoyenneté* on the one hand, and these very human and thoroughly honorable feelings of belonging to a particular place on the other. Happily, the man or woman who exists only as pure intellect has not yet been invented. But love is not earned by merit: love is a gift.

Chapter 11

The State and Political Parties

I. It is laid down in democratic constitutions that the freely elected majority shall govern, while the minority, possessed of clearly defined rights, shall be in opposition. In order that the majority can express its will, we have political parties. They offer manifestos, and a group of people, that the electorate can vote for or against. Since there will always be far fewer parties than there are opinions, the *citoyen* will seldom find a party with which he is in total agreement. So even at the stage of choosing a party he must make a few of those compromises without which no country can be governed. The role of parties, then, is to help voters get their bearings in the political landscape, so that their views are represented in parliament, and the will of the majority is made manifest.

If one could abolish all political parties overnight, but wished to retain free elections and the principle of majority rule, people would immediately form associations that, while they no longer called themselves "parties", would nonetheless take over the same functions. Because any group that tells the electorate ahead of an election "This is how we will run things if you give us a majority" is by definition a political party.

A party is a part (Latin *pars*) of society. Consequently a party that has eliminated or prohibited all other parties is not actually a party at all any more. A party that represents a section of society also participates in the state, in its legislative process, and – potentially at least – in its government. Parties are the transmission belts that link the forces at work in society and the action taken by the state. So their relationship to the state is a matter of some interest. It may seem surprising that parties often give little thought to this. What is less surprising is that parties have very different relationships to the state, depending on their history and their programs.

II. In the Federal Republic of Germany all parties have their difficulties with the state, the more so the smaller they are. The Left Party was founded in June 2007, as a merger of the Labor and Social Justice Alternative (WASG) and the Party of Democratic Socialism (PDS), which is the legal successor to the former state party in the GDR. The PDS did struggle to get used to today's new and very different state, and to accept it as its own. It found this easiest at the local community level, and in regional government. Here it was fully capable of assuming governmental responsibility, albeit not without attempting to combine such responsibility with fundamental opposition to government policy at the national level.

Liberal parties have failed to secure a ruling majority in Germany for more than a century now. The Free Democrats (FDP) have got used to the fact that governing power only comes their way at the national and regional level as the junior partner of one of the mainstream parties. But the big parties are increasingly reluctant to leave the key domestic departments of state to the FDP. The last Federal Ministers of Finance fielded by the FDP held office – both of them only briefly – in the mid-1960s. So back in the time of the Helmut Kohl government this party was able to call constantly for tax cuts, without having to get them through parliament; and in opposition it was able to portray itself as the party that was there for its – largely well-heeled – voters, and not for the greedy state, which was only after their money. The FDP was also the only party that adopted neoliberal principles more or less wholesale. If in the meantime they have performed less well than the Greens in many elections, this is doubtless largely because it is not entirely clear how they intend to govern a state and dismantle it at the same time. At any rate, the Free Democrats appeal mainly to those voters who see the state as a necessary – if not very necessary – evil.

The careers of many Green Party politicians were born of the hatred felt by the student movement for the organs of state, their truncheons and water cannon; the distrust felt by the environmental movement for the authorities, who behaved as if we had another planet in reserve; and the distance that separated the peace movement from the armed power of the state. Consequently many would not accept that there was any difference between a movement and a political party. When Petra Kelly campaigned for what she called the "anti-party party", she meant something which – unlike the "established" parties – did not function as a transmission belt linked to the state. It was not just the Greens who used the term "supportive of the state" as an ironic label for people who had no ideas beyond administering the status quo. For a long time the majority of Greens were not only not capable of governing; they were not willing to govern. All that has now changed completely.

In the country's national and regional parliaments the Greens discovered the opportunities that the democratic constitutional state had to offer them. Like the early social democrats, they were initially interested only in using parliaments as a platform for publicizing their message; but then they noticed that their voters expected more of them. In the end they learned day by day that an ecological reinvention of the economy and society was only

185

possible from a position of government. In order to build an ecological framework for the economy, one had to be in government, preferably in alliance with a mainstream party that at least understood what the Greens wanted.

It may be that the Foreign Minister's slowness in reacting to irregularities in the issue of visas is indicative of a lingering trace of the Greens' earlier detachment from the state. In general, though, the Greens have come to see the state as a real opportunity to influence policy, and not just in the environmental arena. And the days are long gone when they viewed the state monopoly on the use of force as suspect. If they still have to learn the value of this monopoly, and understand that it cannot be taken for granted, then this is something that they have in common with all the other parties. The neoliberal hostility to environmentalism makes the Greens proof against neoliberal contempt for the state.

III. More than other parties, the social democrats are sustained by a long history, which they look back upon with pride. Forming an integral part of that tradition are two periods – each lasting twelve years, as it happens – when the party was persecuted by organs of the state. From 1878 to 1890 it was the Prussian police who broke up meetings of the Socialist Workers' Party or arrested members of its executive, while in 1933 it was Hitler's SA who paraded leading social democrats through the streets on the backs of trucks, with signs hung around their necks, before carting them off to concentration camps. In both cases there were no judges to protect them: in both cases the power of the state was represented, rightly or wrongly, by these minions. In the first case they were acting on the basis of a questionable law; in the second case they were servants of a will that was already above the law.

These experiences have etched themselves deeply into the consciousness of the party. Ferdinand Lassalle had led it to hope that it could take control of this selfsame state with the help of universal suffrage. But the very state that was supposed to help turn disadvantaged workers into *citoyens* enjoying equal rights and social security was intent on destroying their party. This left its mark.

When the collapse of the German Empire in 1918 put government power into the hands of the social democrats, many of them, especially in the regions, did not really know what to do with it. When a social democrat then became *Reichspräsident*, and another briefly served as *Reichskanzler*, many remained skeptical towards a state that continued to employ the same civil servants and officers who had served under the *Kaiser*. They fought against the enemies of the Republic, but this state was never really their own. Until the next, and far more terrible, persecution began.

Konrad Adenauer deserves credit for many things, but one cannot say that he made it easy for the social democrats in the 1940s and 50s to identify with the new Federal Republic. Accustomed to suffering, and sometimes enamored of suffering, outraged social democrats in their assemblies endlessly repeated Adenauer's insult – that electoral victory for their party would mean "the downfall of Germany". If the Chancellor and founder of the state could speak in these terms, then it must mean that the state itself was against them. It took a number of unfazed democrats such as Fritz Erler, Max Brauer, Ernst Reuter, Carlo Schmid and above all Willy Brandt to remind a party battered by constant defeat that "this is your state, which you must help to uphold, and one day govern".

Only when the time was right, when there was a social democrat Foreign Minister and then a social democrat Chancellor, did it become clear to most members of this, the oldest German political party, that despite all the bluster of the election campaign they were no longer outcasts and outlaws, but stakeholders in a respectable constitutional and welfare state, which they all had reason to protect and defend.

What remained, for many, was the subconscious fear that everything could go the same way it already had twice before. The fear fades, but towards the end of the 1980s came the failed attempt to incorporate the simple proposition: "The Federal Republic of Germany is our state" into the Berlin Basic Program and Declaration. So a vestige of ambivalence remains. On a conscious, rational level the social democrats stand full-square behind the state that they helped to found. But in the subconscious, particularly of the older generation, the old fear still lurks.

Most social democrats were immune to the neoliberal *Zeitgeist*. Had not August Bebel had to grapple with the same kind of talk in his day? They will only accept cutbacks in the welfare state if they can see that these are necessary in order to make the social security system viable for the future. And whenever members of the government give the impression that they are trying to make the constraints of globalized markets into their own political program, they are deeply skeptical.

Social democrats with a keen sense of their own history react extremely sensitively when another party behaves as if it is the true, the one and only party of government, as if all is right with the world, and with the country, only as long as power is wielded by the chosen and the elect.

This is the impression created by quite a few christian democrats, and not by accident. The Catholic Centre Party, which was the dominant force when the CDU was founded, had been the real party of government during the Weimar Republic. Nobody could govern without its support. And the various Protestant groups absorbed by the CDU, including elements from the German National People's Party, did not exactly suffer from a political inferiority complex either.

Was not this strong, non-denominational party the only new thing about the party system of the Federal Republic – the only thing that pointed to the future? Was it not the Union of Christian Democrats and Christian Socialists (CDU/CSU) that brought in Ludwig Erhard's social market economy in the teeth of social democratic opposition? And was it not Konrad Adenauer who would not allow anything, not even the dream of German reunification, to dissuade him from incorporating the Federal Republic into NATO, who together with Schuman and de Gasperi paved the way for the European Community and finally got it off the ground? Or at least, that is how post-war history appears to the CDU/CSU. And a lot of this is hard to argue with. It is the result of the fact that the christian democrats and christian socialists had a mandate from the electorate to lead the Federal Republic for the first 17 years of its existence. What another government would have done, what consequences its decisions would have had, is at best a matter for historical speculation. The facts speak for the CDU/CSU, especially as German reunification came about more or less by itself through the collapse of communism, four decades after the foundation of the Federal Republic, without a drop of blood being spilt. The fact that this had something to do with Willy Brandt's policy of *détente* does not materially alter this view of history.

So members of the CDU and CSU have no difficulty in saying what all democratic parties should be able to say: that this state is our state. But a dangerous undertone creeps in as they are saying it: "We built up this Republic, we have always been in the right, and so it can only end in tears if others get to govern the country." The CDU/CSU identifies with the state. And that in itself is a good thing. But it often does so with the unspoken rider: "Therefore what is good for the party is good for the country." Helmut Kohl's imperturbable good conscience in the scandal about illegal party funding, and his posture of moral superiority in the committee of enquiry, are only explicable in these terms. It was his duty to ensure that the right people, not the wrong people, governed the country, and the methods used to achieve this did not much matter. His actions were helpful to the party, and therefore, despite all the talk from legal pedants and nitpickers, they cannot have been wrong. Hence the fact that Kohl, giving evidence before the committee, came up with bizarre arguments after the event to suggest that his opponents were "in breach of the constitution", in order to show that his own breach of the law was necessary and justified as a means of preventing enemies of the constitution from coming to power. Willy Brandt could never have argued in such terms. The former Minister of the Interior Manfred Kanther took the same line before the court as Kohl took before the committee of enquiry: what was good for the party cannot have been wrong.

When the 2002 *Bundestag* elections did not end in victory for Edmund Stoiber, as he had prematurely announced, the CDU/CSU kicked off a campaign the like of which the Federal Republic had never seen. For the first time an opposition questioned, if not the legality of the new government, then certainly its legitimacy. It was "electoral fraud", plain and simple, that had prevented the right party from coming to power. The campaign, which at times recalled the disputed elections that are normal in Asia or Africa, fell apart so ignominiously in a specially convened committee of enquiry that from then on there was no more talk of electoral fraud, especially when it became clear that the Chancellor, contrary to expectation, was able to keep his firm election promise not to send any troops to Iraq.

The basic tenets of what is now known as neoliberalism were so unequivocally denounced in the Papal Encyclicals of 1891 and 1931 that Christian political parties whose programs are founded on Catholic social teaching really ought to be proof against them. That this is no longer the case has to do with the declining influence of the churches on political life, and even more with the pitiful end of communism. In her youth Angela Merkel heard it said a thousand times that communism was winning, and that its laws therefore applied. Whether she ever believed it or not is beside the point. What matters is that communism did not win – and capitalism did. So now the laws of capitalism must apply – and these are formulated by the neoliberals.

Whether she sees herself, as many of her friends see her, as the German Margaret Thatcher is another question. But she must feel a certain kinship with those politicians in Eastern Europe who have replaced the hated command economy with a capitalism that in Western Europe was seen as outmoded. She does not carry the baggage of the debate on principles that has been going on inside the mainstream political parties since the Second World War. In foreign policy and domestic policy her point of reference is the outlook and thinking of the leading power. And today that means the USA. States, as she has learned, can vanish overnight. What matters is whether one has to practice politics under socialism or under capitalism.

IV. Even more important than the relationship of political parties to the state is their relationship to each other. Or to be more precise: their relationship to each other allows us to draw inferences about their relationship to the democratic state.

Those with an overdeveloped need for harmony will always struggle with democracy. Democracy is designed to allow conflicts and disagreements to be settled in public, albeit in accordance with certain rules. Before employers and trade unions applaud the outcome of their negotiations in lofty tones, sometimes even exchanging veiled compliments about their opponent, newspaper readers and television viewers are regaled with stories about how the economy is bound to collapse if the trade unions are not curbed, or how declining purchasing power will drive unemployment up to record levels if management is allowed to have its way.

The consumer of news in a democracy, and even more so the engaged *citoyen*, have to live with conflict, learning in the process what needs to be taken seriously, what half-seriously, and what not seriously at all. The same applies to what party spokesmen say in praise of their own party, or in order to do down the opposition. In nearly all cases a glass of water that is more than half full for the one lot is at least half empty for the others. Those familiar with the game can even derive amusement from it on occasion. But some of the methods used in political campaigning ultimately serve no party's interests, but end up damaging everyone, with democracy and the democratic state coming off worst.

One of these methods is wholesale denigration. It is one thing for the opposition to point out, against a background of rising unemployment, that the government's remedies are clearly not working, and that others must therefore be tried. It is quite another just to say: "The government has failed." Especially when the opposition's economic experts know full well that a different government could not have prevented the rise in unemployment either. So the same game may well be played out again a few years later, but with the roles reversed. The upshot being that a major portion of the electorate regards the mainstream parties as failures one and all.

A wholesale charge of incompetence has the further disadvantage that it renders any detailed discussion of the real issues more difficult or impossible. It is simply not the case that rising unemployment is just the penalty we pay for incompetent politicians, whether they are called Kohl, Waigel, Schröder or Clement. Why is there no discussion about whether, in a mature and sophisticated economy like Germany's, it is still possible to achieve growth rates that so far exceed the mean growth in productivity over the economic cycle that unemployment rates can fall? And about what can be done if this question, based on the experience of the last 30 years, has to be answered in the negative? Why has the head of Deutsche Bank, announcing plans to cut jobs despite high profits, only prompted outrage, instead of a serious debate about how long an economy and a society can live with the principle: "Because the profits of today are never enough, the job losses of tomorrow are the higher profits of the day after tomorrow"? Why are we not allowed to ask the question: "Where are all the new jobs going to come from?"

Sweeping criticism is even more grotesque when it is aimed at national budgets. In Germany public-sector borrowing at every level – national, regional and local – has been too high, regardless of which party was in power. Tax receipts are simply not sufficient to fund everything that the public – rightly – expects government to do. The result is an overall deficit that breaches the Maastricht criteria. When the opposition puts the blame for this on the government of the day, whether in good faith or disingenuously, the effect is to delay or prevent any discussion about what can be done to ensure that local authorities can replace their leaking water mains, that the *Länder* can finance language classes for Turkish children, and that the federal government can build its own motorway tunnels. The fact that political columnists in the serious broadsheet newspapers have not begun to ask how we can end the bidding war between governments in Europe and worldwide for the lowest business taxes is a product of this cheap, generalized criticism, which inevitably rebounds on the critics as soon as they get into government.

V. Even worse than sweeping generalization is moralizing. This reached a new high in Germany following the *Bundestag* elections of 2002. One does not have to be a historian to know that politicians in general – and not only in Germany – have long been accused of lying on a daily basis. This is not the place to expound the thesis that vanity, rather than lying, is the besetting vice of the politician. For this see my book *Die Privatisierung der politischen Moral* (Frankfurt/Main 2000). What is more important is that any party that accuses another of lying puts itself in the dock. Anyone who accuses another of lying will win approval – albeit with the rider: "And you are no better." A politician who accuses the other party of deception will get people nodding in agreement – but he will not convince them that he himself never tells lies. And if he calls someone a hypocrite, he will not be contradicted; but he will encounter people who back him up with a nudge and a wink: "You are right, of course, but then it takes one to know one."

In short, anyone in politics who questions the morality of his opponent – and it happens every day – only damages himself, because he confirms the prejudice which holds that politics in general is a dirty business. But this is not just a party political zero sum game, but a bad habit that parties indulge in at the expense of the democratic state. If a democratic constitutional state lives by the loyalty and commitment of its *citoyennes* and *citoyens*, then the very foundations of this state are bound to be eroded when the impression is created that lies and deceit, deception and corruption are the norm even among democratic politicians.

Surveys have been conducted among voters to find out what they think the government and opposition are capable of, and anyone who studies the results will have to agree that the process of erosion is already far advanced. Those who think only along party political lines will focus on which party is currently regarded as the lesser evil and which the greater. Those who care about the democratic constitutional state will shudder to imagine what will happen when both the major parties have finally succeeded in completely discrediting each other morally.

There is no sign at present that things are getting better, because the rule of thumb states that the smaller the differences of substance between parties, the more liberally the moral indignation gets spread around. These differences of substance are diminishing along with the scope for real policy-making. As the scope for policy-making at the national level becomes ever more circumscribed by the globalization of markets and the directives of the EU Commission, arguments about practicable policy alternatives become more and more infrequent and difficult, and the temptation to escape into generalization and moralizing becomes increasingly hard to resist.

VI. The democratic constitutional state requires and necessitates a political culture in which there can be political opponents, political rivals, but, in so far as we are talking about democrats, no enemies. Perhaps this culture demands that we reflect on the state, on the democratic constitutional state as an overarching value. Only within this state do parties have a function. If they wreck the state, the parties themselves are finished. This state is their state – not their property, but their responsibility. This state can survive the loss of a party here or a party there, but no democratic party can outlive this state. What is good for a party – or at least appears to be good for it – is by no means necessarily good for the state. But whatever strengthens the democratic state is very likely to be good for political parties too.

There is a limit to the strain that can be placed on the democratic constitutional and welfare state. It is resilient, but vulnerable. It is more resilient than many dictatorships, because its *citoyens* can get rid of a government without damaging the state. It becomes supremely vulnerable when its citizens decide that it is not worth the trouble of electing a new government, since it will just obey the same constraints and dance to the same tune as the outgoing government.

This is why the democratic state is reliant on active parties with a strong will of their own and a distinctive character, parties where voters more or less know what they will do in government, and what they will definitely not do. They may – should – have a will to power, and that means a will not simply to acquire the trappings of power. They must not regard themselves as the measure of all things political, as an end in themselves. The laws of the state are above party. A blow to the state is a blow to political parties. And if the state's room for maneuver becomes constrained, parties are the first to be affected.

The nation-state as preserved in the European Union is in a weak position anyway vis-à-vis a globalized economy. That position must grow progressively weaker, the more the standing of politics is diminished. More important than the question of which party is in government is the question of what there is left to govern in such a nation-state, and whether the state, in the interests of the common good and the future viability of its economy, is still capable of establishing a social and environmental framework – or at least working to get such a framework established within the European Union. The prospect of governing a state in which there is hardly anything left to govern can only appeal to people who are vain, attention-seeking and ultimately unpolitical. The task of enshrining the constraints of globalized markets in national legislation can only excite politicians whose consciousness is already "economized".

Serious party politics is politics conducted for a state from the perspective of a party. Therefore all parties have an interest in ensuring that such politics remains possible. This common interest does not supersede the conflict between political parties, but it does override it, and must determine the tenor and tone of the conflict; it must be detectable in that tone.

For all their fierce rivalry, democratic parties do have shared interests in common. Anyone who accuses the other party of being incompetent or even immoral is behaving not only irresponsibly, but stupidly. When the meaning of politics has become so impoverished that people aspire to positions and offices where there is nothing more to decide and nothing more to organize, then the only explanation, apart from ambition, must be a narrowness of vision bordering on stupidity.

VII. General slagging-off of political parties always finds a willing audience. But that is not our present intention. What political parties are, and what they can do, is best seen at the grass-roots level, in local politics. What would Germany be without the thousands of honest and hard-working men and women in our towns and regions, who translate the wishes and concerns of their fellow citizens into local government policies? In the towns and cities at least they are generally members of a political party, but after work they do not read party manifestos: they read budget plans and papers for meetings, or talk to acquaintances who are unhappy about a proposed building development or a parking charge. They are concerned for the well-being of their community. But they are also glad that they belong to a party political group, where they can talk among themselves before they go into the meeting.

Another lesson to be learned from local politics is that our political parties are not too strong but too weak, particularly in terms of their membership numbers. What is a small town to do, especially in the former East German *Länder*, if not enough candidates come forward to fill all the vacancies on the town council? Why are voters in Baden-Württemberg annoyed to find no more candidates on the ballot paper than the number to be elected? They want to make use of their right to move someone up from last place to first by cumulative voting, or to move a good friend from the list of one small party to another by cross voting, and thus get them onto the council. This calls for men and women who are prepared to sacrifice their time and energy for their local community. And such people come predominantly from the ranks of the political parties.

The only time a party gets too strong is when it is able to govern for too long, whether at the local, regional or indeed the national level – and particularly when there is little prospect of removing it from power. This can lead to entanglements and imbroglios that bring not just the party but democracy itself into disrepute.

A really strong party would be one that was able to deliver its message to the majority of the electorate at any time without the media, or through its own media channels. This would mean that political parties would either need many times more members than they have today, or else they would have to run their own TV stations and newspapers. Because all this is out of the question, political parties are far more dependent on the media than the media are on them. When two or three media organizations team up together, they can bring down a politician or a whole party, especially if the rest of the media, obeying a herd instinct, join in the feeding frenzy. Political parties are completely helpless in the face of such attacks.

The real danger is that party membership will continue declining to the point where political parties can no longer function as transmission belts between society and the organs of state, because they only reach very small circles of people. Then parties become what they have long since been in America – election machines, that are switched on when they are needed and switched off again when they threaten to become a nuisance.

This is more than nothing: but it is a good deal less than the European tradition – rightly – demands.

A democratic constitutional and welfare state that is fit for the future needs active political parties that offer the electorate genuine alternatives, and that seek out and train people capable of taking on responsibility for the state at all levels. It is not very convincing when the same commentators who warn against the excessive power of political parties then complain – rightly enough – that they do not have enough members. A democratic republic cannot survive if the very young people who are urgently needed in political life turn away from politics in disgust.

Where this occurs, political parties have good reason to reflect on their relationship to the state and their particular political style. One could wish that the media would subject that style to more frequent critical scrutiny, while at the same time acknowledging and appreciating the substantive work that parties do. If the media too lose their sense of proportion, if they too only value the quick fix, and resort to sweeping generalization and moralizing, either out of laziness or because they have their own political agenda to promote, then the prospects for the democratic state are not good.

Chapter 12

The Future of the State

I. The future of the state, in Europe at least, is bound up with the realization that the 20th century state, the nation-state that exercises sovereignty at home and abroad, has no future.

This tells us two things. First, this is not the end of the line for the state. Without its monopoly on the use of force, the technical civilization of the 21st century is simply not viable. The state is more indispensable now than it ever has been. In Europe the French, the Poles, the Germans, the Hungarians will still have their own state when today's schoolchildren are grandparents. These states will have exactly the same borders that they have today. To that extent they will be more stable than they were in the 20th century. In Germany there will still be a Baden-Württemberg and a Saxony, and the federal *Länder* will have approximately the same functions as today.

The dream of a Europe in which the nation-states would dissolve like sugar in a cup of coffee was largely confined to the Germans anyway. For Britons, Frenchmen, Italians or Spaniards there was never any question of this. The nation-states will not be dissolved but suspended, and therefore preserved.

The European Union will not be a state for a long time to come, but a community of states. Nevertheless it will take on more and more state functions. It will be an important, and in many matters the most important, layer of European statehood. What exactly such a non-state with overriding state functions is to be called is a matter for the constitutional lawyers. For those who struggle with legal definitions, it might be helpful to see the EU as a stable for horses that have for too long been roaming wild across the prairie or trampling through fields of corn; now they have been tamed and turned into workhorses, hitched up to the European wagon – and required to pull it out of the mud if it gets stuck. They are a little weary, and glad, therefore, to have found a sheltering stable: but they are healthy and able to work.

The second thing to be said about the future of the state is that it very definitely does **not** lie in clinging on to, or reclaiming, the competencies and sovereign rights of the traditional nation-state. That future can only lie in relocating elsewhere those functions that the nation-state relinquishes, and must relinquish – to a place where they are more effectively exercised, and with greater promise of success, than in the nation-states. The state has a future if the nation-state is preserved in larger and politically more viable groupings. Or to put it another way, the state can only grow stronger again if first of all it grows weaker. For the groupings we are concerned with here – the most important of them being the European Union – take away from the state rights that were formerly constitutive of it, such as the right to wage war or levy customs duties. But they can also restore to the state spheres of influence that it has already surrendered in the face of a globalized economy: a fiscal policy that accords with its own ideas of justice and the proper functions of a state. For example: only if the European Union can stop states competing to offer the lowest business taxes – which they continue to do – by imposing a minimum of joint fiscal policy will it become more difficult to starve the member states of revenue to the point where they cannot contemplate funding the arts or even implementing social policies.

The state must surrender certain competencies in order to become stronger and more capable of effective action. Only by joining forces with other states can the state hope to combat transnational terror networks, organized criminality that is no respecter of national frontiers, or the privatization of violence. A totally uncoordinated immigration policy practiced by the twenty-seven EU member states would be completely ineffective. A state that sought to protect itself alone against climate change would be a laughing-stock. The fact that the Italian state has been able to survive the open dispute between the government and the judiciary without major signs of falling apart has to do with its integration into the European Community. Citizens of EU states can rely on the fact that certain rules apply in the European Union which cannot be set aside as a result of any upheavals in their own country.

So less sovereignty often means more stability and greater freedom of action. But only if "positive integration" (Fritz Scharpf) does not continue to lag so far behind "negative integration" in the European Union as it has hitherto. If the EU Commission, intent on perfecting competition within the Union, can take exception to the German system of district savings banks; if the Commission can see public-service broadcasting as a form of anti-competitive subsidy, yet at the same time is not responsible for ensuring that large corporations also pay their fair share of taxes; then it takes away from the member states more than it gives them. But this is not because a group of states have decided to form a Union: it is because of the way power and authority are allocated within the Union, and because of the politics of those who run this community of states. Neoliberal politics is always aimed at delivering the – probably imaginary and non-viable – minimal state, whether in Rome, Bratislava or Brussels. Conversely, a politics that regards the constitutional state, the cultural state, the welfare state as indispensable needs to engage with the state at every level, but whether or not it succeeds is decided in Brussels.

What is irritating is not that the Federal Republic of Germany has to surrender more and more areas of jurisdiction to the EU. What poses a danger for the German state is not that German Federal policy and administration find themselves increasingly occupied with enshrining EU directives in national legislation. What must harm the state at the national, regional and local level, however, is the attempt to dismantle the framework put in place for the market and the economy by central government without constructing an equivalent European framework. And if this is encouraged by the distribution of powers between the Commission and the Council, then our political masters must insist upon a change of course.

II. The conclusions that are emerging here from our reflections on the nation-state accord with the views formulated by Ulrich Beck and Edgar Grande in the concluding chapter of their 2004 study *Das kosmopolitische Europa*: "If states want to preserve and enhance their power, they must (a) cooperate, (b) negotiate international rules and (c) establish corresponding international institutions. In other words, because they want to survive, states must cooperate. However, permanent cooperation transforms the self-definition of states from the ground up. Their egoism to survive and to extend their power compels them to unite and transform themselves. National interests are maximized not through rivalry but through cooperation." (Ulrich Beck and Edward Grande, *Das kosmopolitische Europa*, Frankfurt/Main 2004; cited here in the translation by Ciaran Cronin, *Cosmopolitan Europe*, Cambridge 2007, p.254)

Part of this transformed self-definition of the state is also the distinction between "legal sovereignty" and "material sovereignty". Legal sovereignty would include the right to complain at any time about "interference in domestic affairs", which generally implies weakness and insecurity. "Material sovereignty" is embodied in the capacity of the state to do what it needs to do to the satisfaction of its citizens: provide security, protect civil rights, promote sustainability. In the words of Beck and Grande: "Briefly, the state renounces a portion of its legal sovereignty in order to recover its material sovereignty. Even more briefly, and with a paradoxical twist: the renunciation of sovereignty leads to an increase in sovereignty." (ibid., p.78)

What Beck and Grande formulate here as a paradox is not some playful intellectual conceit. It really can work like this in practice, albeit only on condition that EU policy makers want it to. So far the signs are not encouraging. Beck and Grande warn: "A neoliberal minimal Europe does not make economic sense nor is it politically realistic. The economic deficits of an exclusively 'negative integration' of Europe are sufficiently well known. Markets are not only politically constituted but also need continual political correction if they are to function effectively. If such market-correcting policies are not possible at the European level or if they lack support, then not only the European economy but also the European project as a whole will suffer in the long run." (ibid., p.23-24)

According to the authors, right-wing populism could exploit the weaknesses of a minimal Europe. It is clear that the Left would not feel at home in such a Europe, and that it would not keep quiet for ever.

Those who champion a Europe without "market-correcting policies" do not see why Europe should be enabled to do what nation-states cannot do for themselves. They hint that it is quite possible to live in states whose frameworks for markets are falling apart. Where the order of the day is "as little state as possible", it cannot do any harm if a little statehood disappears en route between nation-state and Europe. "This brand of cynicism", observe Beck and Grande, "is typical of neoliberals". (ibid., p.78)

Where the political goal is the minimal state, the necessary and often invigorating surrender of sovereignty by the nation-state can become an instrument for the dismantling of the state. The existence of such tendencies in Europe is unmistakable. Whether they prevail depends on whether or not sufficient political forces can be mustered – and they need not come exclusively from the democratic Left – who want to expect more of the state than neoliberal economists do, and who have moreover understood that European policy makers now decide which matters can still be decided by national governments. If there was such a thing as a European public, which followed what goes on in Brussels and Strasbourg with the same critical attention they give to events in Paris or Berlin, then the formula "the renunciation of sovereignty leads to an increase in sovereignty" could be a description of an actual process. If we then had the debate that Michael Sommer wants to see, about what the state is for and what it should be doing, this might well assist the cause of "material sovereignty". The latter really can be restored by a structure that, like the European Union, embraces an entire continent, even if it is not itself a state, and therefore cannot claim any "legal sovereignty". What this structure would have to accomplish in the way of positive integration is evidently already being discussed in a series of special committees subordinate to the EU Commission.

III. Naturally the state's capacity for action must also be strengthened from within. This is achieved not by employing more civil servants, but by persuading citizens everywhere to identify with the state and take ownership of it. For this to happen they must have the opportunity to understand who is responsible for what, and therefore who can be held to account for what. This is particularly difficult in a federal state like Germany. Why has the construction of a bypass been put on hold? Because Germany's Federal government, which is responsible for trunk roads, has more urgent priorities? Or because the regional planning authorities are not making any headway? Why is a particular law that one has been waiting for not yet on the statute books? Who is right, when both chambers of the German parliament, the *Bundestag* and the *Bundesrat*, each blame the other?

In a general election – for the *Bundestag* – the electorate is asked to make a judgment on what the government majority has achieved or failed to achieve. If the opposition has been using the *Bundesrat* to co-rule or to block government action, how can the electorate tell who is responsible for what? For this reason the much-touted reform of federalism in Germany is long overdue. It is not just a question of speeding up the legislative process, but also of giving the electorate a clearer overview and understanding.

To remind voters more often that the democratic state is their state, we need the plebiscite. Everybody is familiar with the arguments against plebiscites, some of them long since refuted, others irrefutable. Of course a plebiscite can result in a decision that is flawed or wrong. But that can happen without a plebiscite. And of course plebiscites – just like elections – create opportunities for demagogy on the part of interested media organizations.

On the other hand, decisions made directly by the voter carry more weight. They cannot be altered or blocked by lobbying government ministries or parliament, and industry associations cannot cherish the hope that an early change of government will reverse the decision. It is easier, and less dangerous, to indulge in unbridled polemics against a parliamentary majority decision than to launch a verbal assault on a referendum. It is easier to run down a government than a majority of the electorate.

Another consideration is this: how are we to foster an awareness in the *citoyen* that the democratic constitutional state is **his** state, and not the state of some "political class", if the people described in these rather polemical terms do not trust voters to reach sensible and rational decisions? The democratic state draws its legitimacy from the responsible adult citizen. In future it will have even greater need of such legitimation if it is to stand firm in the face of globalized economic power. Those who insinuate that the *citoyenne* and *citoyen* are less than competent to make decisions are needlessly weakening a state that is already weakened.

The authors of a carefully drafted bill which has been submitted to the German *Bundestag* have gone to great lengths to guard against any abuse of the referendum process, including the initial petition for a referendum. Since members of parliament were involved here, they have taken care to ensure that the plebiscite is used to complement, extend and enhance parliamentary democracy, not replace it. Why have the media commentators who like to threaten our incompetent and useless political parties with the plebiscite now fallen strangely silent when these same parties are now prepared to risk the plebiscite themselves?

IV. The realization that even the best nation-state, left to its own devices, is utterly helpless in the "world risk society" (Ulrich Beck), applies not only to the small and medium-sized states of "old" Europe, but also to the really big states such as China and India, and even to the hegemonic power of the day, the USA. The unilaterally declared and unilaterally fought "war on terrorism" was bound to fuel terrorism. The only way to fight terrorism successfully is by getting the police forces and secret services of all the major powers to work together. The capacity to defeat any enemy in a real war by military means alone is not a great deal of use if a war, even a war that has been won, costs more in political capital and money than it brings in. Even the most powerful economy cannot survive without international cooperation, especially if it relies on foreign investors to finance the massive deficits in its budget and balance of payments day after day.

In a mutually interdependent world, even the nation that is by far the strongest pays a high price for withdrawing from the common endeavors of the community of nations, and possibly sabotaging them. The fact that the United States wants nothing to do with the Kyoto Protocol or the International Court of Justice has incensed so many people around the world that such hostility to the superpower cannot be a matter of complete indifference to the US State Department.

Roman emperors not infrequently behaved according to the motto *oderint dum metuant* ("let them hate me, just as long as they fear me"). This was in an age when despots need only fear the dagger or sword, or possibly poison. And they had their bodyguards and food tasters to deal with these threats. In the 21st century, which has to live with suicide bombers who blow up themselves and others, who turn passenger jets into flying bombs, nobody, and no nation, can afford the luxury of such a cynical maxim. Anyone who arouses fear or hatred, trusting in his own superior might, will have a price to pay. Presidents can be protected by preventing them from mingling with the crowd, or by locking down whole cities ahead of their visit. Millions of tourists cannot be protected.

When the twin towers of the World Trade Center collapsed, the Americans were awakened from the dream of invulnerability. George W. Bush believed that America is entitled to this dream, and his fellow countrymen have thanked him for it. That vulnerability is a part of the human condition, and that people cannot make themselves invulnerable, was already known to the creators of the Nibelungen saga, who caused the linden leaf to land on Siegfried's back, so that a "window of vulnerability" remained open. But never before has the dream of invulnerability proved so naïve, so costly, so dangerous and so counter-productive as a political maxim as it has in the 21st century. Somebody who actually goads thousands of fanatics into demonstrating his country's vulnerability is wasting the billions that have been spent on a missile defense system.

V. The mutual dependency of countries in the 21st century also explains the interest that each has in the statehood of the other. In the wake of 11 September 2001 many Americans have regretted that the US simply abandoned Afghanistan to itself, its warlords, its Muslim fanatics and its drug dealers as soon as there were no more communists to fight there. Bin Laden was able to train his terrorists there unmolested. In the meantime everyone has learned that when states fall apart, when the police – assuming the country still has a police force – are more interested in exacting road tolls than in fighting crime, when the writ of the interior minister – assuming the country still has one – does not run beyond the city limits of the capital, then trouble is brewing that will put neighboring countries, and eventually other states far away, at great risk.

Implicit in the proposition "because they want to survive, states must cooperate" (Ulrich Beck/Edgar Grande) is another: "If states wish to survive, they need other states in order to do so", or to put it another way: "States that wish to survive have an interest in the statehood of all others." And they share this vital interest because the disintegration of statehood affects us all.

The fact that statehood can vary greatly in quality, that dictators exploit their state as if it were their own private property, that others behave like warlords, that whole areas of state activity can collapse while others do not – all this begs the question: which is more likely to succeed, a strategy of gradual change, of democratization and legitimation, or a strategy of *tabula rasa* – sweeping the board clean and starting from scratch again? Both options are arduous and time-consuming, but that does not excuse us from giving an answer. The responsibility for giving an answer rests primarily with the affluent countries of the northern hemisphere, who call the tune in the United Nations. And the answer is likely to be: wherever it is possible to avoid the *tabula rasa* option, it should be avoided.

If the first priorities for the northern hemisphere are to prevent the dismantling of the state and to get the democratic constitutional and welfare state into a shape and a context that allow it to survive the 21st century, then the task confronting Africa, Latin America and parts of Asia is to arrest the acute decay and collapse of states, to prop up fragile states, and to rebuild states that have fallen apart.

There are several reasons why politicians are not anxious to grasp this particular nettle. For one thing, nearly all the efforts undertaken so far have proved ineffectual, questionable, misguided or counterproductive. And for another, those regions where the state is falling apart are generally not of any economic interest. Just as, in the eyes of neoliberal capitalism, millions of people in the industrial nations are no longer needed, so whole countries, indeed continents, can become surplus to requirement. Where global capital no longer invests anyway – and with good reason – it is not interested in the state as such.

So it is mainly scientists and academics, and the development aid policy makers who listen to them, who press governments to come up with strategies. And sometimes the pressure comes from ministers of the interior, who are worried about security in their own country, and who get alarmed when there is no longer a telephone number they can call in one of these faraway lands.

VI. The most serious attempt so far to draw up some guidelines for this whole intractable area has been made by Tobias Debiel, Stephan Klingebiel, Andreas Mehler and Ulrich Schneckener in their policy paper of January 2005. They are well aware that there is no such thing as a universal remedy for these problems. So they start by surveying the territory, and are at pains to demarcate and classify: "On the one hand are countries like Mexico, Brazil, Thailand or South Africa, that approximate to the Western model of democratic market economies, while at the same time often being unable to offer their citizens the protection they need against threats to their life and livelihood (failure of the security agencies to deal with high levels of common crime, lack of basic social security to cushion against economic shocks, etc.). At the other end of the spectrum are collapsed states – an extreme that has so far only manifested itself in a few cases (e.g. Somalia, Afghanistan, Liberia, Sierra Leone). The majority of countries are somewhere in the middle, between these two poles. They are classed either as insufficiently unified – or 'weak' – states, where legal certainty, protection against violence and a social infrastructure are only partially present; or as 'failing states', which are already in decline, and which could end up by collapsing altogether." (Tobias Debiel, Stephan Klingebiel, Andreas Mehler and Ulrich Schneckener, *Between Ignorance and Intervention. Strategies and Dilemmas of External Actors in Fragile States*, Bonn 2005, p.4)

For our four authors, then, state collapse begins at the point where, on the fringes of mega-cities like Rio or Sao Paulo, the number of victims of gang crime and gang warfare in a single year approximates to the strength of a 20th century army division on a full war-fighting footing. For the authors, the citadels in which the well-heeled barricade themselves when the police no longer control the *barriadas* or *favelas* are the first signs of state collapse. Yet the state still exists, with elected presidents, and laws that remain in force throughout the greater part of the land. But there is none of that at the other end of the scale, in the *entités chaotiques* that are not only *ingouvernables*, but indeed *ingouvernées*.

Most states, according to the authors, are somewhere in between, and the closer they are to collapse, the more necessary – and the more difficult – it becomes to intervene from outside.

Our authors also warn against the illusion that a quick fix is possible: "In general fragile statehood should not be seen as the exception – a deviation from the norm represented by the typical OECD state – but rather as the rule in many parts of the world." (ibid., p.4)

Lest anyone should suppose that they are falling back on a kind of post-modern relativism, intimating that a functioning state is not really necessary any more, they go on: "This is not to question the long-term significance of the OECD model as a normative-historical ideal. But such a view is an acknowledgement of the fact that the worldwide establishment of liberal democracies and stable state structures within the next few decades is not a realistic prospect. The multi-layered reality of fragile statehood rules out any 'one size fits all' solutions." (ibid., p.4)

If we want to arrest the process of state collapse and strengthen and legitimize states, then we need to think in terms of decades.

And if we want to fashion a state out of an *entité chaotique*, we need to think in terms of generations. The probability that mistakes will be made, that what will be achieved is the opposite of what is desired, is greater than the likelihood of rapid success. Reviewing what has been accomplished so far, the authors come to a damning conclusion: "A phase of all-out actionism is often followed by an abrupt about-turn, which then gives way to a mood of conscious passivity. Somalia is the extreme example, but the same zigzag progression can be observed in the case of Haiti, Burundi or the Democratic Republic of Congo. The erratic sequence of turning a blind eye, tactical maneuvering, intervention and then turning a blind eye again is likely to be especially unhelpful in situations where the need is to strengthen structures in fragile states for the long-term." (ibid., p.3)

This zigzag course derives in part from the fact that the policy sections of our foreign ministries have for a long time failed to take the issue of state collapse seriously, and consequently have not prepared any strategies to deal with it. The whole point about foreign policy is that it is conducted between states. Where there are no states, there is no foreign policy. Now, according to the authors of the policy paper, there is a "renaissance of the state in academic study and practice". But this is not enough. Hence the recommendation: "The federal government needs integrated, cross-departmental structures for action on foreign policy, security policy and development aid policy, in order to be able to react effectively to the problem of fragile statehood." (ibid., p.11)

This of course applies not only to the German government, but to the European Union and its key member states. In the past it has been the case that the different government departments have ploughed their own furrow, particularly those responsible for defense and economic cooperation. But there are situations in which development aid policy must pass, because no minister is prepared to dispatch aid workers into an inferno of violence, or to authorize credits when nobody can any longer guarantee that they will be used correctly. Conversely the military has learned that while it can put an end to the shooting and the killing, it cannot create peace or make development happen. So it is high time that both departments of government – along with the foreign ministry – agreed on common strategies.

VII. The biggest difficulty here is that a state can only be strengthened or rebuilt from within, through its own citizens, so that the provision of outside aid needs to be handled very delicately. Identifying who are the right "elites", who can do what needs to be done, is often difficult. Who has the interests of the state at heart, and who is looking only to his own advantage? Should one rely on those who are – nominally – in government, or on those who call themselves the "opposition"? An extremely complicated set of recommendations reflects the difficulties in which anyone who tries to formulate guidelines here necessarily finds himself: "Official state structures that have forfeited their legitimacy have no right to receive better support than equivalents that function effectively and possess a minimum of legitimacy."

What purports to be legal is by no means necessarily legitimate. And someone who rebels against a corrupt regime is not *ipso facto* proof against corruption himself.

Although no state can be constructed without a minimum of security, it is not enough just to attend to the police and justice system. As long as judges and police officers can only feed their families if their salaries are supplemented by bribes, then the reform of the public finances also needs to be addressed by such a strategy. Just as there can be no economy without a state, so there can be no state without an economic foundation.

Anyone who studies the difficulties and the sometimes impossible dilemmas inherent in what Francis Fukuyama calls, with excessive optimism, "state-building", will bear failed attempts in this area with equanimity and celebrate any successes with gratitude. What is clear, certainly, is that all such attempts are doomed to failure unless they can avoid the taint of colonialism. This rules out unilateral action. In the absence of a legitimate monopoly on the use of force, only duly authorized force can fill the gap in the short term and reconstruct such a monopoly on the use of force over the long-term. Where, as in Iraq, a global power has crushed a tyranny contrary to the will of the UN Security Council, it must reckon with privatized counter-violence. This counter-violence will always be directed likewise against those who seek to create a new legitimacy under the protection of the superpower.

Anyone who sets out to create legitimate national monopolies on the use of force, and hence nation-states embedded in the international community, must be able to invoke an international monopoly on the use of force.

The idea of such an international monopoly on the use of force is not new. It inspired the founding fathers of the United Nations. The decision whether to use force was to rest with the UN Security Council. This, it was thought, would prevent wars between states. Our world is still a long way from that. But the idea that a UN monopoly on the use of force must replace the *jus ad bellum* claimed by individual states is still the right way to go.

Now there is another argument to support this view. Where national monopolies on the use of force start to crumble, they can only be saved or restored if they can be propped up, and if necessary temporarily replaced, by a force whose legitimacy is beyond doubt. Any unilateral intervention is motivated by self-interest – or so say the despots who have filled the vacuum left behind by the state. A global police force, legitimized and dispatched by the community of nations, is above such suspicion, even though it is necessarily made up in the first instance of units made available by individual nation-states.

Every state order starts from the distinction between legitimate and illegitimate force. And unless we wish to abandon large sections of the planet to warlords or bands of marauding killers, it is a distinction we need to insist upon. This means that legitimacy must be accountable. Where different armed factions claim legitimacy with threadbare arguments, the result is the kind of chaos in which ordinary people, including women and children, become fair game for a brutalized soldiery. Only where a certain emblem – and it does not have to be a blue helmet – signals that the international community is intervening does privatized and commercialized violence become illegitimate and – if it will not submit – criminal violence.

Of course the UN Security Council, whether it is enlarged or not, does not make its decisions in an interest-free zone. The interests of the great powers may encourage a particular intervention, or more likely prevent it. So perhaps we should think about setting up a – purely advisory – board of "elder statesmen" and experienced legal experts, which could draw up and publish recommendations. Such recommendations might cover such matters as when, in general terms, intervention is necessary and legitimate. Or they might relate to specific trouble spots, such as western Sudan. Now that the focus has shifted from the definition of a "just war" to concerns about the legitimate use of force, the authority of the Security Council needs to be underpinned and backed up, but also critically scrutinized, by persons who have earned our trust and are above any suspicion of sectional interests.

Such suggestions may appear unrealistic. And of course no such body can come into being if the United States is opposed to it. But once governments begin to grasp the notion that the failure and collapse of statehood has become the central issue in peace policy and development policy at the start of the 21st century – and probably not just at the start of the century either – then one way or the other they will have to come up with some new ideas.

VIII. The threats to statehood in the affluent northern hemisphere are different, and less dramatic, than the threats it faces in the more or less impoverished south. This is why they have been discussed separately in the present chapter. But they are not unrelated to each other. Knowing what is going on in Africa or Central Asia changes the way we read reports about our own country. If German policemen threaten to work to rule in a protest about poor pay, inadequate equipment or slow promotion, it all sounds harmless enough. This is the standard rhetoric of pay negotiations. Then we recall that the acute collapse of states in Africa starts when the police, paid a pittance, lose interest in protecting street markets and catching criminals. Whereupon traders hire their own private protection squads, who mete out their own brand of violent justice, and stage public executions to deter criminals. West Africa is a long way from Central Europe, of course. But might the gap not narrow in time?

When a senior German executive whose company is taken over by another receives a golden handshake that yields enough in interest alone to pay the salaries of half a dozen German Chancellors, it leaves most people on normal salaries speechless, because they just cannot imagine such sums. If anyone dares to criticize, they are promptly accused of being motivated by envy. But in our present context we need to ask whether it is good for a society in the long run if senior business executives are paid ten, thirty or fifty times more than their counterparts in the public sector. Might this not become a source of corruption, leading ultimately to state collapse – as in Latin America?

Do the gated communities in the US have different implications for the state's monopoly on the use of force in Brazil and South Africa than they do in the US? Or is it just the case that there are citizens in all three countries who isolate themselves because they prefer not to rely on the security offered to them by the state? Can a state stand by and watch with impunity while security becomes a commodity? Does the privatization of violence, wherever and in whatever form, not ultimately damage the very core of the state?

There is a further nexus to be considered here. Many states in the southern hemisphere need the attention and assistance of the north in order to survive. The indifference with which Europe and North America have tolerated or even ignored the atrocities going on in the Congo or on its eastern borders, in Rwanda and

Burundi, is easy to explain, but hard to excuse. To create a functioning polity again out of such a vast *entité chaotique* demands sacrifices of those who attempt it, sacrifices of money – lots of money – and lives. It is not enough to put a few thousand soldiers on the ground to check the worst excesses in a city and the surrounding region. What is needed, as we have seen, is a meticulously planned long-term commitment, both military and civilian. It is not just a matter of neutralizing the warlords, or of weaning thousands of child-soldiers off killing and teaching them about work. It is a matter of organizing all the things that make the state preferable to the warlords: public benefits such as certainty of the law, schools, water and electricity, food for the helpless, and a police force that knows what it is for, and takes its job seriously.

IX. Accomplishing all this is by no means child's play for Europe, even with the cooperation of the US. It is also open to question whether the level of financial aid to the countries of the southern hemisphere is sufficient, given that delivery has fallen increasingly short of the target figure of 0.7 per cent of national product promised to them for the past 35 years. At stake here is our own security too, which is entirely dependent on the security of others; and anyone who has understood this knows that the peoples of Europe can deliver what is required – look at what they managed to do when they were at war with each other! – but only if their states remain capable of action.

The resource-starved state, which is not even capable of stopping the race to offer the lowest business taxes, will certainly not be able to deliver. It will provide a token amount of aid. When the images become too horrible to look at, people will donate a few millions, and from time to time they will send a few troops and hope that they will be home again in time for Christmas. But the process of state collapse will continue until the consequences are plain for all to see, even in Europe. By which time it may well be too late for many countries in the southern hemisphere. Once violence has been totally privatized, it cannot just be renationalized like a run-down rail network.

The state – and not just the nation-state as preserved within the European Union – has a future, provided we really want it and plan for it. And we want it if we do not view the democratic constitutional and welfare state as something to be taken for granted, something that can stand any amount of stress and strain, or indeed as something tiresome or restrictive. It is one of the greatest achievements in the history of mankind.

We want this future if we do not deceive ourselves about the alternative. For that would be a future without security, without law, without basic rights, without the practice of freedom.

We, the children of a technological civilization, in which everything rapidly becomes obsolete and consigned to the scrap heap, find it hard to imagine that there are areas of life that do not obey the laws of the throwaway society, because a better way of doing things is not apparent, or perhaps even possible. It will always be necessary to adapt the democratic constitutional and welfare state to new circumstances – or in other words, to reform it. But it cannot be replaced by something better. Because a better way of doing things has yet to be devised.

Postscript

On Our Way to the Market-State?

I. The modern state has a long history. It goes back to the medieval emperors of the Hohenstaufen dynasty, more specifically to the Sicily of Frederick II in the 13th century. Other historians structure this history differently, beginning with 15th century Italy. One of them is Philip Bobbitt, who deals with a special aspect of this history in his book *The Shield of Achilles: War, Peace, and the Course of History*. But Bobbitt, although a professor, is no ordinary academic historian.

Bobbitt has served as a senior adviser in the White House, the Senate and the State Department, he has held several posts in the National Security Council, and most recently he was the senior director for strategic planning in both Republican and Democratic administrations. At the same time he was a member of the Oxford Modern History Faculty.

The title of his book *The Shield of Achilles: War, Peace, and the Course of History* does not even hint at what may surprise readers: Bobbitt the historian tells us the story of the modern state, while Bobbitt the expert in strategic planning links this story to changes in military technology which in turn were bound to change military strategy. So we learn how military requirements produced new kinds of state: the "princely state" (1494 – 1648), the "kingly state" that merged into the "territorial state" (1648 – 1776), the "state-nation" (1776 – 1914), and the "nation-state" in what Bobbitt calls the "Long War" (1914 – 1990). How far this analysis is valid and persuasive is a matter for historians to debate. What is interesting in the present context is Bobbitt's conclusion: just as the state-nation had to be replaced by the nation-state, so the nation-state, in the 21st century, will be superseded by what Bobbitt calls the "market-state". It does not matter whether Bobbitt likes or recommends this market-state (he does). Whether we like it or not, this new type of state is what history will bring about.

There are many good reasons for the decline and the "disintegration of the legitimacy" of the nation-state: "No nation-state can assure its citizens safety from weapons of mass destruction; no nation-state can, by obeying its own national laws (including its international treaties) be assured that its leaders will not be arraigned as criminals; no nation-state can effectively control its own economic life or its own currency; no nation-state can protect its culture and way of life; no nation-state can protect its society from transnational perils, such as ozone depletion, global warming, and infectious epidemics." (Philip Bobbitt, *The Shield of Achilles: War, Peace, and the Course of History*, New York 2002, p.228)

II. The market-state, of course, cannot do this either. But this type of state does not even claim to do it. It is not the task or the ambition of the market-state to be able to do all this. The market-state is more modest – and perhaps more honest.

This new modesty is even more apparent when it comes to social responsibility: "Whereas the nation-state justified itself as an instrument to serve the welfare of the people (the nation), the market-state exists to maximize the opportunities enjoyed by all members of society. For the nation-state, full employment is an important and often paramount goal, whereas for the market-state, the actual number of persons employed is but one more variable in the production of economic opportunity and has no overriding significance. If it is more efficient to have large bodies of persons unemployed, because it would cost more to the society to train them and put them to work at tasks for which the market has little demand, then the society will simply have to accept large unemployment figures." (ibid., p.229)

What the market-state has to offer for its citizens is opportunity: opportunity in all its forms, economic and cultural. The best instrument for creating opportunities is the market. So the market-state is no longer directly responsible for people, but for the markets that will supply opportunities. Citizens have to turn to the markets, they have to seize the opportunities offered by the markets. And if they do not, it is their own fault.

"In the era of the nation-state, the state took responsibility for the well-being of groups. In the market-state, the state is responsible for maximizing the choices available to individuals. This means lowering the transaction costs of choosing by individuals and that often means restraining rather than empowering governments. Thus we see measures like the proposal to limit the percentage of GDP taken by government, and other forms of capping the tax rate." (ibid., p.230)

How far should governments be "restrained"? The answer is: much more radically than in any of the other types of state described by the historian Bobbitt: "If the nation-state was characterized by the rule of law the market-state is largely indifferent to the norms of justice, or for that matter to any particular set of moral values so long as law does not act as an impediment to economic competition." (ibid., p.230)

So does this mean that what promotes competition is good, what impedes competition is bad? In addition to the market-state's indifference to the norms of justice, Bobbitt notes its "essential indifference to culture". (ibid., p.230) And he seems to know what this may mean: "The sense of a single polity, held together by adherence to fundamental values, is not a sense that is cultivated by the market-state." (ibid., p.230)

There is no lack of frankness in this book. But what else should hold a society together? Is it the "forthcoming motto" Bobbitt proposes – "making the world available" – which he explains in terms of "creating new worlds of choice and protecting the autonomy of persons to choose"? (ibid., p.233) This autonomy to choose includes genetic manipulation: "Shifts from a passive acceptance of inherited abilities to a quest for the enhanced, or engineered, faculties made possible by molecular biology." (ibid., p.232)

This, of course, would not hold together societies with a Christian and humanistic tradition. On the contrary: it would tear them apart. But it could serve to promote competition and economic growth. In fact competition could now begin long before people are born.

III. The scope of state activity and of political decision-making in the market-state must shrink considerably. Education? Anyone can buy education by sending his children to a private school. Good education, of course, will necessarily be expensive. Parents will know what they can afford. Social security? Anyone can look up the telephone numbers of insurance companies; the competition between them will create customer opportunities. Personal safety? Protection against crime? The security business is booming, and supply will always grow to meet demand.

So Bobbitt can imagine what government might look like: "Is governance easier in the market-state, because so much less is demanded of it, or more difficult because the habits of the good citizen are lost? Perhaps both. Contemporary political reporting is not presented against an historical background of complex competing values, but increasingly in terms of the power relationships of the personalities involved, as if politics were like a simple sporting event – who is winning and who is losing, or, as shown by the little arrows in a popular news magazine, who is up and who is down. This is characteristic of the market-state, with its de-emphasis on the programmatic and legalistic aspects of governance. And is this not what politics is in the market-state?" (ibid., p.231)

So politics is just a game played by people who like it. They can win, they can lose, but this does not make much difference to the rest of society. Politicians may be elected, not to influence or change society, but to protect and promote the markets. And these markets – including the labor market – will determine the individual's quality of life. What is left will at best be politics without policy. Politics animated by policy will not be forbidden, but it will be an exercise without an object, no longer impinging on actual events.

This is what Bobbitt has in mind when he comes to define the role of the citizen: "The role of the citizen *qua* citizen will greatly diminish and the role of citizen as spectator will increase." (ibid., p.234) It might be fair to add: it is not only his role as spectator that will increase, but also his role as client. As a client he (or she) will have plenty of opportunities. Even as a spectator they will be clients of the media, and the media will deal with matters formerly covered by the government or opposition. But the classical *citoyen* and *citoyenne* responsible for the common good will either vanish or become figures of ridicule.

If we stick to Max Weber's definition of the state, the market-state is no state at all. There is no longer a monopoly on the legitimate use of force, neither internally nor in foreign relations. Protection against crime can be purchased in the marketplace, and even wars can be privatized: interventions could be executed by "voluntary coalitions of essentially mercenary forces, compensated by contributions from all states having a stake in the outcome". (ibid., p.803) Using the mercenary market will be a matter of collecting money.

Bobbitt is fully aware of the fact that in the 21st century there will be different forms of private or privatized violence. In

223

common with other American strategists he prefers the term "low-intensity conflict": "If, as Martin van Creveld speculates, 'the day-to-day burden of defending society from low-intensity conflict will be transferred to the booming security business,' this mixture of devolution and privatization will become commonplace in the market-state." (ibid., p.237)

Privatized force against privatized violence? The experience of Latin America, or even of the United States, does not augur well for this kind of conflict. Very often the methods of fighting on both sides tend to become alike. So Bobbitt adds: "This is a harrowing prospect, but one with which we may have to learn to cope." (ibid., p.237)

IV. Philip Bobbitt is a citizen of the United States. In his book he never tries to disguise this. When he uses the pronoun "we" he means "we Americans". In one of the last pages of his book he refers to the "long overdue defense review under the direction of Andrew Marshall. Its recommendations were the focus of intense scrutiny and, like the proposals in the present work, many of which they resemble, were controversial." (ibid., p.814)

So in an article in the *New York Times* of 10 March 2003 Bobbitt supported the attack on Iraq, arguing that "the Iraqis would be much better off after an invasion". "Better off" is an interestingly ambiguous term, covering the spectrum from material wealth to social/political/economic health. Are we to take it that "better off", here, means closer to market-state democracy? Bobbitt does not like the European Union and fears that if it "were to persist in its current course, it would be attempting to thwart the emergence of a market-state". (Philip Bobbitt, *The Shield of Achilles: War, Peace, and the Course of History*, New York 2002, p.234) Thus only the United States "is remarkably well situated to become a market-state". (ibid., p.242) Although George W. Bush could be regarded as a champion of the market-state – and American voters trusted him twice – even the United States is still some way off achieving that status. Bobbitt is convinced that American leadership will promote the market-state. But he realistically doubts whether states like France, Germany, Japan, South Korea, Taiwan or Singapore will follow the American example.

So he assumes that there will be three different types of market-state: the "entrepreneurial market-state" (the one that is fully compatible with his definition of the market-state); the "mercantile market-state" (he cites the East Asian tiger states as examples); and the "managerial market-state" (which he equates, surprisingly, with the *soziale Marktwirtschaft* model developed in the Federal Republic of Germany). Much of what Bobbitt describes as mercantile or managerial market-state is inconsistent with his original definition of the market-state, so Bobbitt sometimes rightly uses the terms "mercantile state" and "managerial state". (ibid., p.673) Ludwig Erhard's *soziale Marktwirtschaft* developed more than half a century ago has nothing to do with Bobbitt's market-state.

The state which, according to Bobbitt, will be and should be the result of the "Long War" is the "entrepreneurial market-state". The other types are a concession to a reality which might prove persistent and even obstinate. The model that Bobbitt outlines is the state that has to serve the market, and that transfers to the market much of what hitherto had been the privilege of the state. Bobbitt's message is a state which will transform the citizen into a client. It is a new, perhaps a revolutionary message.

V. To take it seriously does not mean that we must expect to wake up some day in a flawless market-state. This seems rather unlikely not only for us, but for our children too. Even the United States will never become a perfect market-state. Much less will this happen in Europe. In the five years since the publication of Bobbitt's book, Europe has not moved closer to the market-state: on the contrary. The principle of privatization is no longer taken for granted. Politicians have discovered that privatization needs more regulation, not less. The state's responsibility for social security is no longer questioned by political parties who want to win elections. The indispensable tasks of the state, a taboo in 2002, have become a topic of serious discussion.

Aside from this new trend there are reasons why the market-state is unlikely to come, and even more unlikely to stay. The first reason is that most people do not want it and will not put up with it. Modern democracy is based on, and lives by, the principle that the citizen is responsible for his state, and the state is responsible for its citizens; that the citizen has to support his state, and the state has to care for its citizens, especially those who are most in need. Modern democracy has inherited the duty to guarantee security and to protect citizens from any kind of violence. To this it has added the task of providing and organizing social security. There is plenty of discussion about how all this is to be achieved. And there will be more in the future. But whoever tries to abolish the principle is bound to fail. There is no majority – and there will be none – in favor of transforming the citizen into a client. Just as there was no majority for Lenin's new man transformed by communism.

There is another reason. Even if powerful media persuasion could create such a majority, the market-state will not be sustainable. A state that is "indifferent to justice" and just accepts and trusts the results of market competition will have to cope with the fact that the gulf between the rich and the poor deepens from year to year. But this cannot go on indefinitely. At a certain point the society will be split. There are slums, where criminal gangs successfully challenge the police; and there are gated communities, fortresses within the cities, where people who can afford it pay for their security. Privatized (criminal) violence produces privatized (protecting) force. But in the long run – as the experience of Latin America shows – privatized force turns into violence, too. Chaotic violence inevitably leads to the decay of any state: in fact it is part of that decay. And the market, as Bobbitt knows, needs a state.

University professors can imagine all kinds of states, even extremely weak ones. But reality does not admit and tolerate every kind of state. A state must be viable. In order to be viable it must at least try to meet the expectations of its citizens. It must win the loyalty of these citizens by catering for their needs and aspirations, their hopes and their fears. Any state that refuses to do this will not prove viable. The market-state, at least in Europe, will not come about, because it is at odds with the European tradition, at odds with the very idea of European democracy. Wherever the media might succeed in persuading a majority to try it out, the market-state is likely to perish. In a worst-case scenario its demise could entail the demise of the state itself.

VI. All this notwithstanding, Bobbitt's *The Shield of Achilles: War, Peace, and the Course of History* is a valuable contribution to political debate. Those who criticize the modern welfare state are always very clear when they tell us what the state should no longer do, what the state should leave well alone. They are less forthcoming on the question of what the state should continue to do. They are very eloquent in explaining why private initiative is superior to state interference: but they are reluctant to define where state action is indispensable.

So we do not know – and perhaps the critics themselves do not know either – what kind of state might be left if neoliberal thinking were to prevail. A "lean" state sounds good. It may indeed be desirable. But what does "lean" mean? What is the term telling us – or not telling us? Philip Bobbitt puts an end to vagueness, to doubts and uncertainty. The market-state is a plausible consequence of the political ideology that began to become hegemonic after the implosion of the communist system. What started with Ronald Reagan and Margaret Thatcher will culminate in the market-state. Bobbitt: "The emergence of the market-state has not occurred in an instant but rather over a couple of decades. Within the most prominent market-states, the groundwork was laid by Margaret Thatcher and Ronald Reagan, who did so much to discredit the welfare rationale for the nation-state." (ibid., p.339)

Every ideology that wants to create a new world needs an element of Utopia. Just as Marxism tried to inspire the working class by the vision of a classless society in which the needs of everybody will be met, Bobbitt's market-state shows the adherents of Friedrich August von Hayek and Milton Friedman what kind of new world they can create. Just as Marx did not praise the classless society as a political goal to be reached by a political party, but as the natural course of history, something that was bound to come as part of an inevitable process, so Bobbitt does not recommend the market-state as his goal, or even as the best state possible, but rather as the natural outcome of the process he has described in more than 500 pages. What began in the 15th century with the "princely state" will, in the 21st century, reach the stage of the market-state. Just as Marx told his followers – and his opponents – "whether you like it or not, this is what will happen", Bobbitt says: this is how history will answer the questions posed by the changes that have occurred during the Long War. The difference might be that Marx claimed a scientific method, and consequently a scientific truth. Both men refer to laws or at least to rules of history, and both have discovered these laws or rules not by intuition, but by what is taken seriously in the modern world: many years of hard scientific work.

VII. So let us ask why the market-state is necessary, why it is the only possible – and reasonable – answer to the changes wrought by the Long War. Bobbitt begins with a very conventional argument, which is still important and difficult to refute: The "state exists to master violence: it came into being in order to establish a monopoly on domestic violence, which is a necessary condition for law, and to protect its jurisdiction from foreign violence, which is the basis for strategy. If the state is unable to deliver on these promises, it will be changed; if the reason it cannot deliver is rooted in its constitutional form, then that form will change. A state that could neither protect its citizens from crime nor protect its homeland from attack by other states would have ceased to fulfill its most basic reason for being." (ibid., p.216)

This applies to any state. It is the reason why the "princely state" came into existence. And it is the reason why the nation-state, according to Bobbitt, is no longer viable: "The strategic innovations of the Long War will make it increasingly difficult for the nation-state to fulfill its responsibilities. That will account for its delegitimation. The new constitutional order that will supersede the nation-state will be one that copes better with these new demands of legitimation, by redefining the fundamental compact on which the assumption of legitimate power is based. Three strategic innovations won the Long War: nuclear weapons, international communications, and the technology of rapid mathematical computation. Each has wrought a dramatic change in the military, cultural, and economic challenges that face the nation-state. In each of these spheres, the nation-state faces ever increasing difficulty in maintaining the credibility of its claim to provide public goods for the nation." (ibid., p.215 ff.)

These strategic innovations, about which Bobbitt knows much more than his critics (including the author of the present book), prevent the nation-state from doing what any state has to do in order to justify its existence: to "protect its homeland from attack by other states". Nobody can refute this. But if the nation-state can no longer deliver security – and every state has to do this – is there any other type of state that can? The market-state? With mercenaries and a booming security business? Bobbitt does not make such a claim. What he does assert is that the market-state "copes better with these new demands of legitimation", not by more effective means of defense, but "by redefining the fundamental compact on which the assumption of legitimate power is based". (ibid., p.216)

The market-state does not deliver security – and it no longer claims to do so. But the market-state, as a state, will thus "have ceased to fulfill its most basic reason for being". The market-state, according to Bobbitt, is not better suited to protecting its population. Where it differs from its predecessors is that it does not pretend to protect anybody. It renounces its responsibility for security. But where, then, will legitimation come from? From its promise to maximize opportunity? If the state, as Bobbitt concedes, "exists to master violence", this legitimation will not be enough – and not only for those people who, for various reasons, cannot profit from maximized opportunities.

There are people who would like to dispense with the state. They believe that in the absence of the state the markets will thrive and mankind will finally be free. Bobbitt is not one of them. He maintains that the state is necessary. And he repeats that what he expects – and recommends – is not a market, but a state promoting the market. However: the state that he envisages here does not even meet his own criteria for defining the state – however minimal.

VIII. The classless society predicted by Karl Marx was an extremely attractive vision. It created optimism and self-confidence in the working class. So who will be inspired by the vision of the market-state? There will be – and there are – people who are fascinated by the prospect. But most of them already adhere to neoliberal thinking. And most of them are likely to live in Anglo-Saxon countries, especially in the United States.

For others it will have a sobering effect. They may have agreed with those who feel that the state should be leaner, with less bureaucracy, that it should not intervene everywhere. Now they have been shown what this may lead to. And if they consider what it may mean for their personal life, they may well doubt whether they will be among the beneficiaries of the new market-driven order.

And there will be many, especially in Europe, who will be grateful to Philip Bobbitt. Because he has put into words what they definitely do **not** want. They will be increasingly skeptical when they are told that the market is always more intelligent than politicians, and that individual freedom must increase wherever and whenever state activity decreases. And perhaps, certain in the knowledge of what they reject, they will look more closely and more constructively for an acceptable alternative.

In 2005, when most of this book was written, those who were searching for such an alternative were a negligible minority. As we move into 2009, it looks increasingly as if they might become a majority. For amidst the current flurry of bank nationalizations and government bale-outs across the world, a common theme is emerging: it is the state, so stridently written off for so long by so many, that is now having to intervene to prevent financial markets and reckless bankers from ruining the world economy. Even in America, the heartland of the neoliberals and neoconservatives, it is the state that is now stepping in to shore up the banking system and restore confidence in the markets. So what was, back in 2005, the informed surmise and deep-seated but unfashionable conviction of a few, has been vindicated by recent events: even the markets, it turns out, would not be well served by the market-state. No less than society as a whole, the market needs a functioning state capable of effective action.

References

Albrecht, Renate, *Paul Tillich Gesammelte Werke*, Stuttgart: Evangelisches Verlagswerk, 1956.

Beck, Ulrich (translated by Patrick Camiller), *What is Globalization?*, Cambridge: Polity, 2000.

Beck, Ulrich, Edgar Grande (translated by Ciaran Cronin), *Cosmopolitan Europe*, Cambridge: Polity, 2007.

Bobbitt, Philip, *The Shield of Achilles: War, Peace, and the Course of History*, New York: Random House, 2002.

Debiel, Tobias, Stephan Klingebiel, Andreas Mehler, Ulrich Schneckener, *Between Ignorance and Intervention. Strategies and Dilemmas of External Actors in Fragile States*, Bonn: Series Policy Paper of the Foundation of Development and Peace, 2005.

Enzensberger, Hans Magnus, *Aussichten auf den Bürgerkrieg*, Frankfurt am Main: Suhrkamp, 1993.

Eppler, Erhard, *Die Privatisierung der politischen Moral*, Frankfurt am Main: Suhrkamp, 2000.

Eppler, Erhard, *Vom Gewaltmonopol zum Gewaltmarkt*, Frankfurt am Main: Suhrkamp, 2002.

Esping-Andersen, Gøsta, *Why we need a new Welfare State*, Oxford: Oxford University Press, 2002.

Fukuyama, Francis, *State-Building: Governance and World Order in the 21st Century*, Ithaca, New York: Cornell University Press, 2004.

Göhler, Gerhard, Matthias Iser, Ina Kerner (eds.), *Politische Theorie. 22 umkämpfte Begriffe zur Einführung*, Wiesbaden: Vs Verlag, 2004.

Haller, Gret (translated by Alan Nothnagle), *The Limits of Atlanticism. Perceptions of State, Nation and Religion in Europe and the United States*, Oxford/New York: Berghahn Books, 2007.

Hayek, Friedrich August von, *Law, Legislation and Liberty: A New Statement of the Liberal Principles of Justice and Political Economy Vol. 2, The Mirage of Social Justice*, London: Routledge and Kegan Paul, 1976.

Kersting, Wolfgang, *Theorie der sozialen Gerechtigkeit*, Stuttgart: Metzler, 2000.

Kurtenbach, Sabine, Peter Lock (eds.), *Kriege als (Über)Lebenswelten. Schattenglobalisierung, Kriegsökonomien und Inseln der Zivilität*, Bonn: Dietz, 2004.

Menzel, Ulrich, "Der Zerfall der postkolonialen Staaten", in: *Aus Politik und Zeitgeschichte*, Vol. 18-19/2001.

Morini, Martin, "Historischer Kompromiss: Berlusconi und die Mafia", in: *Blätter für deutsche und internationale Politik*, No.3/2005.

Münkler, Herfried (ed.), *Lust an der Erkenntnis: Politisches Denken im 20. Jahrhundert*, Munich/Zurich: Piper, 1994.

Naumann, Friedrich, *Die politischen Parteien*, Berlin: Buchverlag der Hilfe, 1910.

Orwell, George, *Nineteen Eighty-Four*, London: Penguin Books, 1989.

Reinhard, Wolfgang, *Die Geschichte der Staatsgewalt. Eine Vergleichende Verfassungsgeschichte Europas von den Anfängen bis zur Gegenwart*, Munich: Beck C. H., 2001.

Ruf, Werner, *Politische Ökonomie der Gewalt: Staatszerfall und die Privatisierung von Gewalt und Krieg*, Opladen: Vs Verlag, 2003.

Scharpf, Fritz W., *Regieren in Europa*, Frankfurt am Main: Campus, 1999.

Schmidinger, Thomas, "Sudan – Der Staat als Warlord", in: *Blätter für deutsche und internationale Politik*, No.2/2005.

Shaw, Martin, *Theory of the Global State*, Cambridge: Cambridge University Press, 2000.

Tocqueville, Alexis de (translated by Henry Reeve), *Democracy in America*, New York: D. Appleton and Company, 1899.

Vogel, Hans-Jochen, Heribert Prantl, *Politik und Anstand – Warum wir ohne Werte nicht leben können. H.J.Vogel im Gespräch mit H. Prantl*, Freiburg: Herder, 2005.

Weizsäcker, Ernst Ulrich von, Oran R. Young, Matthias Finger, *Limits to Privatization: How to Avoid Too Much of a Good Thing*, London: Earthscan Publications, 2005.

Willke, Gerhard, *Neoliberalismus*, Frankfurt am Main: Campus, 2003.

www.ingramcontent.com/pod-product-compliance
Lightning Source LLC
Chambersburg PA
CBHW020608270326
41927CB00005B/226